AMERICAN
COZY

AMERICAN
COZY

HYGGE-INSPIRED
WAYS TO CREATE COMFORT & HAPPINESS

STEPHANIE PEDERSEN

STERLING
New York

STERLING
New York

An Imprint of Sterling Publishing Co., Inc.
1166 Avenue of the Americas
New York, NY 10036

ISBN 978-1-4549-3035-8

Distributed in Canada by Sterling Publishing Co., Inc.
$^c/_o$ Canadian Manda Group, 664 Annette Street
Toronto, Ontario M6S 2C8, Canada
Distributed in the United Kingdom by GMC Distribution Services
Castle Place, 166 High Street, Lewes, East Sussex BN7 1XU, England
Distributed in Australia by NewSouth Books
45 Beach Street, Coogee, NSW 2034, Australia

For information about custom editions, special sales, and premium and corporate purchases,
please contact Sterling Special Sales at 800-805-5489 or specialsales@sterlingpublishing.com.

Manufactured in China

2 4 6 8 10 9 7 5 3 1

sterlingpublishing.com

Cover design by Elizabeth Mihaltse Lindy
Interior design by Gavin Motnyk
Illustrations by Mitch Blunt

To my dear husband, Richard Joseph Demler, and our beloved sons: Leif Christian Pedersen, Anders Gyldenvalde Pedersen, and Axel SuneLund Pedersen. You are my favorite American family!

CONTENTS

INTRODUCTION

WHAT IS AMERICAN COZY?

Americans are welcoming people. We love to use—and share—our time, our resources, and our homes.

I call this American cozy. It's a celebration of our unique brand of comfort, personality, and togetherness.

I was introduced to American cozy when I moved as a child to the United States from Canberra, Australia, where my parents had been living, working, and attending university. Our first American stop was the small Nevada town of Logandale, near the Arizona and Utah borders. This was the home of my mother's parents, the Hutchings family. Their house, though overfilled with furniture and mementos, felt friendly. It was crowded with a mix of antique and new furnishings. Each room—from paint to flooring—was a different color. Each table and shelf displayed a mix of knickknacks. Framed family photos, religious sayings, oil paintings of the desert, and needlepoint hangings competed for space on each wall (even the garage and storage shed walls). The oversized chairs and sofas were draped with homemade afghans. And, best of all, their home was perfumed with the permanent aroma of pot roast and chocolate chip cookies.

If they weren't cooking or eating, cleaning or wandering around outdoors, my grandparents and anyone else who was visiting would congregate in the living room, sitting on the sofas and chairs, using the organ and piano benches as seats, or (usually the kids) reclining on the shag carpet. Together, we'd talk, watch television, play checkers, or even nap, as my grandparents would sit in their matching recliners and read scripture (my grandmother) or crochet (my grandfather).

Ever since then, I have thought fondly of American homes. The colors, knickknacks, and aromas may change depending upon the lives inside, but the homes remain places of warmth, comfort, and togetherness, decorated in the trimmings of lives well lived. In fact, from the stories my American friends tell, the Hutchings homestead wasn't that much different from their own families' homes.

And there's a good reason for that. We Americans love places and things that feel inviting. Our sofas, for instance, must actually feel great

to sink into. Our artwork has sentimental value. We like photographs. We adore showcasing our signature style, and we enjoy weaving personal interests into our space (be that our home, our yard, our car, or our office). Whether it is using mounted guitars as art, hanging a homemade quilt on our office wall, or painting a garage door with chalkboard paint so our kids can display their artistic skill, most American spaces comfortably show off their owners' personalities.

American cozy is picnics, multigenerational walks around the neighborhood at sunset, barbecues, and pool parties. It's field days, chatting with neighbors over the hedges, holiday dinners, and houseguests. It's brunch, happy hour, and lemonade sipped on the porch. But we struggle to find the time for these elemental pleasures. In fact, Americans' collective Achilles' heel is "too much": too much stuff crammed into spaces, too many activities, too many obligations, too much to do. We are so overscheduled that, while we have fond childhood memories of these comforting activities—and we deeply desire to make them part of our daily lives—few of us are able to enjoy them today.

Despite the frenzied, adrenaline-fueled world we live in, many of us can't shake the feeling that there must be a slower, more magical, more comfortable way to get by in the world.

Speaking for myself, for years my life looked like most everyone else's life: get up, get the kids ready for school (frantically looking for keys, a son's missing tie, lost homework…), dash to work, get the kids, make dinner, clean, help with homework, do laundry, prepare for the next day, shower, go to bed. Wake up. Repeat.

Then one day I woke up and realized that I did not love my home, my work, my schedule, or even my life. All of these were crammed full of stuff: appointments, activities, and obligations that meant nothing (or very little) to me. I thought back to my childhood and remembered the quietude I had experienced when I looked out a window, weeded our kitchen garden, made cookies with my friends, or stretched out on the living floor to watch television with my siblings.

In an effort to retrieve some of that peace, I stopped answering my phone, texts, and emails. I avoided social media platforms. I said no to assignments that didn't pay well. I told my kids they could be in either the school chorus or the local opera company's fall performance. I set aside a 30-minute family cleanup period each evening so I wouldn't be spending precious time folding laundry all by myself. And I started using my slow cooker.

All this cutting back helped immensely. But even as my life became less frenzied, it still didn't exactly feel peaceful. So I went deeper, experimenting with "lifestyle systems" from other countries. First I played with feng shui, the ancient Chinese art of right placement. Then I tried the Kondo method of living that is so popular in modern Japan. And while these practices helped my home feel clean, clear, and more livable, they did not create those feelings of warmth and calm that I so craved.

I could not shake the feeling that there must be a slower, more magical, more comfortable way to get by in the world. This is when I remembered my father's Danish family and their light-filled, uncluttered home, their love of easy traditions, and the feelings of warmth and comfort I always felt when I visited them.

Their house wasn't fancy, nor was it large. But it was airy and light, with a feeling of tranquility. The floors were blond wood. The walls were yellow-beige with white trim. Ornaments were few. The light came not from a plethora of lamps (as it did in most American homes I visited), but from uncovered windows and, at night, candles. The house was perfumed with roast pork, butter-sautéed apples, and cardamom. Meals there were slow and unrushed. There was enough of everything, but not so much to create clutter. Noise and silence coexisted comfortably. There was something about life in this home that felt both cozy and expansive at the same time.

As it turns out, my father's family members were not the only ones who had found a way to wrap a clean and uncluttered life with a deep sense of contentment and warmth—this was a characteristic of Denmark itself.

If you're not familiar with this small northern European nation, it can help to know that Denmark is the happiest nation on Earth. At least that's what the *World Happiness Report 2016* states. This tiny Scandinavian country—known for pastry, political cartoons, statuesque blondes, and sleek modern furniture—has been found by the authors of the report to have the most personal connections between citizens, overall health, education, social services, charitable giving, benevolent government,

and average income of any of the world's countries. All of which—again, according to the report—lead to happiness.

Danes themselves agree with this assessment. But, they quickly add, there is something the report forgot to mention: the uniquely Danish idea of *hygge*. Pronounced *HEW-guh*, it's an ancient concept that Danes use to spin their love of comfort into a lifestyle.

GET TO KNOW DENMARK

Here are some fun facts about one of the world's coziest countries:

- Approximately 5.7 million people live in Denmark.

- The Copenhagen harbor in Denmark is clean enough to swim in.

- There is no word *please* in the Danish language.

- Lego® blocks are a Danish invention. The word is a combination of Danish words *leg godt*, meaning "play well."

- Fifty percent of people living in Copenhagen ride a bicycle to work each morning.

- Denmark's wind turbine industry is huge; more than 40 percent of Denmark's energy supply is produced by windmills.

- Copenhagen's Strøget, at almost 2 miles (3.2 km) long, is the oldest and longest pedestrian street in the world.

- The world's oldest (Dyrehavsbakken) and second-oldest (Tivoli) amusement parks are in Denmark.

- Because of its small size, no matter where you travel in Denmark, you will never be more than one hour, or 50 kilometers (31 miles), from the ocean.

JUST HOW HAPPY ARE THE DANES?

Danes are the happiest people on Earth. Literally. At least if you believe the *World Happiness Report*, which ranks the happiness of each of the world's countries. Denmark took the top spot in 2012, 2013, and 2016, and came in third in 2015. (The authors did not issue a report in 2014.) In 2017, Denmark came in second behind its Nordic cousin, Norway. Another Scandinavian country, Iceland, was third.

The *World Happiness Report*, which ranks the happiness levels of 155 countries, studies the business and economic health of a country, how engaged its citizens are in civic causes, the communications and technology available to citizens, diversity, what social issues concern its citizens, education levels, family life, physical and mental health of the population, the country's environmental policies, energy sources, hunger and shelter, the state of the government, public safety, religion, infrastructure, access to transportation, and employment. To read current and previous reports, you can visit http://worldhappiness.report.

While hygge cannot be described in a single English word, it can be explained in several. Hygge is experiencing quiet joy in any given moment. It is the complete absence of anything annoying or emotionally overwhelming. It is taking pleasure from the things around you. Like the Danes themselves, *hygge* is a practical word, one that encourages you to create beauty in your daily interactions, objects, and activities. It is the Danish ability to spin the functional into an almost spiritual experience. It is the magic of turning any situation into a moment of coziness.

Think of hygge as a kind of a Danish law of attraction meets feng shui with a dash of positive thinking—all snuggling near a warm fire while wrapped in a down comforter. Fortunately for those of us in the US, hygge is the perfect complement to our unique comfort culture. It is also the perfect antidote for America's culture of "too much."

It sounds almost too good to be true, doesn't it? When I first committed to applying hygge to my overstuffed American life, I didn't know what to expect. Would the Danish-style uncluttered walls or the well-edited calendar or the more streamlined weekday dinners even be possible for me and my family? Were a fireplace and a bunch of candles all I needed to give my house the same warmth and magic of my father's childhood home? Would holidays celebrated in a contained, homemade way even work here? Could I focus more in some areas in order to gain more time and freedom in others?

After several years of implementing hygge (often imperfectly), I am happy to say that my life has been forever changed. People comment on how calm I am, how I get so much done, how warm my home feels, how sensible and centered my children are. Much of this is true—I am calmer than ever. My kids are unruffled. I do get more done in a smaller amount of time. My home does feel warmer. It's almost as if by magic.

We Americans want this magic. And we can get it—easily—by implementing simple changes in our homes, schedules, and offices. We'll start by exploring what coziness is and why it's so important to our overall happiness. Then we'll move on to how you can use the Danish principle of hygge to cozy up every single part of your life—from your schedule to your work life, your home to your holidays. You'll even try on easy ways to use hygge to upgrade your personal style. Along the way you'll find tips for creating hygge for yourself, simple recipes for comforting and nourishing meals, and a paradigm-shifting way to "hyggeify" your world by changing your relationship with time.

Grab a cup of coffee (or tea). Light a few candles. Snuggle into your favorite chair. Queue your favorite music (at a gentle, low volume). Let's dive in and learn the Danish art of "right living"—what it is, why it works, and how to use it to improve your life. You'll be amazed at how wonderful your life can be.

AMERICAN
COZY

CHAPTER ONE

COMFORT:
THE FOUNDATION OF COZINESS

C omfort is important to humans. Physically and emotionally, comfort creates a feeling of safety and warmth that helps humans thrive—you included.

It is also the foundation of both America's unique brand of coziness and the Danish concept of hygge, the gratitude Danes have for everyday items and activities, and the joy they find in each moment.

If you've never given comfort much thought, play a memory game with me. Think back to the last time you were uncomfortable—physically, socially, emotionally, mentally, or in any other way. Maybe you were wearing shoes that pinched your feet, or you got caught in the rain and were stuck on a crowded subway with wet clothing. Perhaps you kept replaying the embarrassing moment you entered a networking event with the back of your skirt tucked into your control-top pantyhose. Or maybe you experienced something more or less serious, or just different.

Cozy: a feeling of comfort, warmth, and relaxation
"A cozy cabin tucked away in the trees"

Synonyms: snug, comfortable, warm, homelike, homey, homely, welcoming, safe, sheltered, secure, down-home, homestyle; informal: comfy, toasty, snug as a bug (in a rug)

Whatever caused your unease, there is a good chance that it left you struggling to focus on anything but your distress. Your thoughts may have taken a dark or angry turn. You may have snapped at someone. You may have become less patient and less good-humored.

For most of us, the ache passes and life returns to normal (until the next time). But for whatever reason, some people don't shed their agitation, and it becomes a defining part of their personality. No doubt you've met people worn down by life's irritations, who are irate, quick-tempered, judgmental, moody, unlucky, self-entitled, and unpleasant.

On the flip side, you probably know people of good character. My father used to say that living through adversity is a character-building opportunity for those brave enough to learn about themselves and the world through their unease. These are often people who have experienced great loss or live daily with physical or emotional pain—people who are wise, brave, magnanimous, grateful, patient, open-minded, and of reasonably good cheer.

My point? Comfort is a choice that can have less to do with the size of our own daily annoyances and tribulations and more to do with how we choose to see and appreciate what we have. In this chapter, we'll discuss how to celebrate the life-affirming power of comfort and how to create comfort for yourself and your loved ones.

"Consider any individual at any period of his life,
and you will always find him preoccupied with
fresh plans to increase his comfort."

—Alexis de Tocqueville

CHOOSING COMFORT

Many of us go along each day feeling a range of emotions—from sadness to boredom to annoyance to happiness—based on what is happening to us in any given moment. Someone bumps into us on the sidewalk and we may feel annoyance or fear for hours afterward. A compliment from someone we admire may leave us smiling for days.

What do our emotions have to do with coziness or the Danish practice of hygge? Choosing your emotions is a mindset trick that is at the very foundation of a comfortable life. And it is something Danes are brilliant at.

I'll explain a bit more. Humans are capable of an enormous range of emotions—in fact, many of us experience a wide span of highs and lows in any given hour. But the feeling of comfort—a gentle, focused way of going through life—has a hard time coexisting with these emotional ups and downs. They are distracting and break our focus from the good we have in our lives.

Biology is also at play here. Fluctuating emotions prompt our adrenal glands to flood our bodies with cortisol, which artificially amps up everything from our heart rate to our body temperature and stimulates our nervous system to function above its normal baseline. All of this is helpful when you are trying to outrun an attacker or think your way through a sales presentation, but a body on high alert is a body that cannot be truly comfortable.

So how do we modulate our emotions? Here are a few tricks to get you started.

Make gratitude your brain's default place. It is nearly impossible to feel anything but comfort when you're in a place of gratitude. What is good in your life that you can feel lucky about? If you can't think of anything, I'll start you out with a few. You've got a body that gets you through the day. You woke up this morning. You have fun, hopeful things called desires. (After all, if you're reading this book, you desire something more for your life!)

Notice one beautiful thing about every person who crosses your path. When you easily notice good things about other people, it becomes more difficult to live in a place of negativity. Your brain is simply too busy looking for good to dwell on the bad. For years I was a life coach, and one of the exercises I asked all clients to do was to find something beautiful about every single human they saw. Give it a try with the people you see—from the woman behind you in the checkout line who is loudly gossiping on her cell phone to the angry subway rider yelling expletives to his fellow passengers. Maybe all you can find beautiful about them is their taste in shoes, or their surprisingly good hair, or their graceful fingers. Just find something! This exercise sounds so simple that you'll be tempted to skip it. Don't. It's easily the most powerful exercise in this entire book and will give you two important skills: the calming ability to find good anywhere and a deep sense of peace. Do it for an hour. You'll feel exhausted, but also powerful and centered. Continue for a day, another day, and another, and your life will change for the better.

Stop complaining. How long can you go without complaining—either aloud or in your head? Every time you complain, you are telling yourself (and anyone who is willing to listen) that you are not comfortable with something in your life. Eventually your brain is going to agree that there is no comfort in your life. Your sense of ease and peace will be enormous once you stop telling yourself and everyone else what is wrong in your life.

Say thank you. Have you ever held a door open for someone—excited to do something kind—only to have the person breeze by you without even looking at you? Or spent time to find the perfect gift for someone, only to receive a tepid response? It feels terrible, doesn't it? Avoid making another person feel this way by saying thank you.

Always. It keeps your heart and your mind in a place of gratitude, which is the best place to be if you want to enjoy a cozy life.

Celebrate small victories, as well as mid-sized and large ones. Celebrating good things is a way of saying thank you to whatever or whomever (yourself included) has given or helped you achieve something. A celebration is a festive thank-you. It is the ultimate act of gratitude. The celebration does not need to be elaborate or time-consuming (unless you want it to be). It can be as simple as blocking out half a Saturday to go to the zoo alone or buying a cookbook you've had your eye on. Anything that would make an effective bribe for yourself would also make a perfect celebration.

Limit media. It is difficult to feel calm and happy among today's headlines, especially when you mull them over for hours on end. While you cannot end world drama and suffering, you can ensure that your focus and well-being are not compromised by limiting the media you consume each day. Your brain will be clearer. Your heart will be more open. And you will feel more focused and grounded without the drama and trauma swirling around in your head—and without the cortisol your body pumps into your system as a result of obsessing over media stories.

Try a social media fast for two weeks—or indefinitely! A social media fast entails taking a break from Facebook, LinkedIn, Pinterest, Instagram, Snapchat, Twitter, YouTube, chatrooms, and any other virtual arena where people come together to connect, brag, gossip, tear others down, seek validation, show off their bodies or wealth, boast about their kids, complain about their bosses, and so forth. Social media is a wonderful way to connect with people who aren't in your everyday life, but it comes with a dark side. Studies have shown that daily use of social media detracts from face-to-face relationships, reduces personal investment in meaningful activities, increases one's sedentary behavior, encourages internet addiction, and weakens self-esteem through unfavorable social comparison. In one recent study, published in the February 1, 2017, issue of the *American Journal of Epidemiology*, researchers recruited 5,208 adults and tracked their Facebook activity for two years. Among their many findings are that individuals who consistently "liked" others' content or clicked links found in Facebook posts showed a significant reduction in self-reported physical health, mental health, and life satisfaction. If you think you cannot live without social media, try two weeks without it. I can tell you from experience that stepping away for a bit will leave you feeling calm, centered, empowered, and very comfortable.

Find time for charitable works. My Danish grandmother used to remark that only people who don't have enough to do spend time creating trouble for themselves and others. There may be any number of reasons why you thrive on chaos or negativity, but one effective way to upgrade your behavior is to spend time each week on charitable works. From the ASPCA to Meals on Wheels to local park cleanups, being of service gives you the opportunity to see that you are vastly more important to the world when you are assisting others than when you are spinning your wheels creating craziness for yourself and those around you.

Get professional help if you need it. If you find that you have trouble seeing the good in your life and in others, or if you feel depressed or anxious, consider finding a professional to help you feel more calm and comfort. You are worth this investment.

DO SOMETHING!

Just as letting life play with your emotions is bad for your comfort level, passively waiting for life to happen to you is also damaging.

Passivity is an urge or learned tendency to live at reduced speed, to gravitate toward whatever takes the least effort (even growing annoyed when asked to do something that requires energy), and to opt for doing nothing, even when you really want something. This can leave you feeling negative, depressed, and checked out of projects, relationships, activities, and your own life.

While, on the face of it, passivity appears to be related to that cozy state we're celebrating here, it can actually make it hard to create and enjoy coziness. Passivity is not "being chill" or kicking back and relaxing. Passivity is aggressively doing nothing and allowing life—or anything else—to do everything for you.

Think about it this way: you can take your chances and let your mood or the day's events determine your mood, or you can be clear about choosing what you want to feel—a sense of comfort—and then set about proactively feeling that way, as well as looking at areas of your life that you can change to bring about a greater sense of ease and comfort.

"Life is really simple, but we insist on making it complicated."

—Confucius

THE WHEEL OF HYGGE

Scandinavians know that real comfort comes not from zoning out or passively letting life pass you by, but from diving in, enjoying life's experiences, and creating a workable balance (notice I said "workable" and not "perfect") between the different areas of our lives.

Living mindlessly—or the flip side, bingeing on certain experiences—is the antithesis of coziness. It deadens our nerves and makes us less present, less focused, and less able to notice if our lives feel out of whack, all of which can erode the quality of our lives.

Scandinavians believe that life's many facets must be in balance if you want to enjoy hygge. To help you discover more about what is and isn't working in your current life, I present to you the wheel of life—a standard in the self-improvement world and one of my favorite tools for pinpointing areas of your life that could benefit from an overhaul.

This popular life-coaching tool features eight sections. Look at each section on the opposite page and place a dot on the line marking how satisfied you are with each area of your life. A dot placed at the center of the circle or close to the middle indicates dissatisfaction, while a dot placed on the periphery indicates ultimate happiness. When you have placed a dot on each of the lines, connect the dots to see your wheel of life.

If this were a bicycle wheel, how smooth would your ride be?

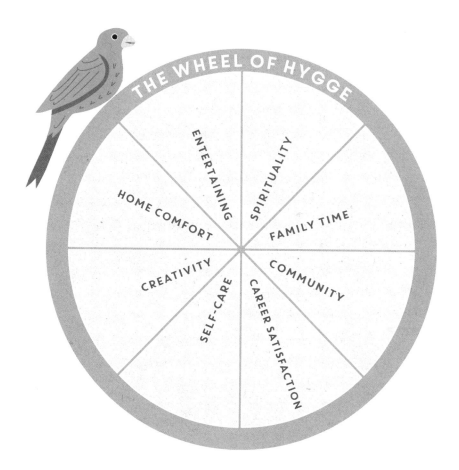

THE WHEEL OF HYGGE

ENTERTAINING
SPIRITUALITY
HOME COMFORT
FAMILY TIME
CREATIVITY
COMMUNITY
SELF-CARE
CAREER SATISFACTION

If you recognize that there is an imbalance in your life, there is a chance you will do something about it rather than trying to numb or distract yourself with excess activity.

Choosing to be comfortable, overcoming passivity, and tackling areas of your life that can impede comfort—all of these contribute to the American cozy mindset you'll want in place as you move further into this powerful, joyful, ease-filled, life-changing journey.

CHAPTER TWO

EASY DOES IT:
WHY CALM MATTERS

One of the most difficult parts of living a cozy life has nothing to do with getting rid of possessions, moving your furniture around, or managing your schedule. It is being calm.

In chapter 1, we talked about the importance of choosing coziness and pursuing physical and emotional comfort without hesitation. In today's "go get 'em!" world, the word *comfort* is seen by some as a synonym for lazy, low-energy, fearful of change, or idle—someone who is more concerned with feeling good than being productive. In the world I grew up in, however, comfort meant none of these things. Instead, the word *comfort* described actively accepting the things, people, activities, and circumstances in our life—seeing each of these things positively and deriving joy from them (either a gentle, quiet appreciation or a huge, gratitude-fueled euphoria).

Before we move on to the physical tools we can use to create a cozy life, there is one more mindset you'll want to tackle: calmness. Yes, calm describes a quiet room, an ocean without waves, or a sleeping baby.

But it means so much more, especially to Danes. Here is the meaning of *calm* that I grew up with: the absence of nervousness, agitation, anger, negativity, or distraction. Without being (and feeling) calm, you will have difficulty consistently creating calm—no matter how much decluttering, smart scheduling, or feng shui-ing you do.

THE SCIENCE OF CALM

Scientific research underscores the importance of staying calm to your health and your overall life. Here are just a few examples.

Stress shrinks your brain. Research has found that stressful events— such as a job loss, death, or relationship problems—can reduce the gray matter in the medial prefrontal cortex, an area of the brain that regulates not only emotions and self-control but also physiological functions such as blood pressure and glucose levels. Further, brain scans of individuals who have undergone recent sudden traumas have found a shrinking in the part of the brain that controls emotional awareness. As this part of the brain withers, we may start to lose touch with our emotions and act in inappropriate or even unfeeling ways in our interactions with other people. Ongoing stressful situations, such as living with a chronic health condition, were shown to affect the brain's mood centers, skewing our ability to regulate pleasure and reward and leaving one susceptible to mood disorders, such as anxiety. And chronic day-to-day stress may leave individuals more vulnerable to brain shrinkages in key areas when a sudden life trauma or ongoing situation does happen.

"It was only from an inner calm that man was able to discover and shape calm surroundings."

—Stephen Gardiner

Stress may be related to tumor risk. Studies have found that stress induces signals that cause cells to develop into tumors. The culprit is a cancer-signaling process called JNK, which—when activated by environmental stress conditions—travels throughout the body, one cell at a time.

Reducing stress can heal your brain. Researchers have found that 45 minutes or more of daily meditation increases the cortical thickness in the hippocampus (the area of our brains that governs learning and memory), as well as in certain areas of the brain that play roles in emotion regulation and reducing self-referential processing. This last term is a fancy way of saying you take everything personally. For example, if your boss is short-tempered, you fear she doesn't like you instead of considering that something may be going on in her own work or personal life. Daily meditation also was found to decrease brain cell volume in the amygdala, which is responsible for fear, anxiety, and stress.

Not sweating the small stuff translates to a longer, healthier life. Researchers have found that a positive mood in the face of stressful situations reduces the inflammation throughout the body that can make a person vulnerable to heart disease, cancer, obesity, joint diseases, immune system disorders, and other conditions. New research suggests that keeping small annoyances from influencing one's mood can play a significant role in one's long-term health.

HOW TO KEEP CALM AND CARRY ON

Most people agree that keeping your cool in the face of minor annoyances, mid-sized irritations, or even monumental inconveniences or dangers is admirable. And if you want to create a cozy life, learning how to be calm is something you'll want to master. It is impossible to truly live in the spirit of hygge when you are being sidetracked by uncomfortable emotions. But it can be difficult to keep calm and carry on.

Even those of us who are biologically wired for calmness—or raised in a family that actively instilled calm in us—can struggle with being cool and collected in all areas of our lives. I am unruffled by deadlines, meeting new people, getting to unknown places, being alone or in a group of strangers, speaking in front of others, or being near snakes or dogs. But put me in a room with two or more whiny children and it takes every ounce of willpower I have to keep my composure. I've even been known to cross streets (against oncoming traffic, no less) when walking in front of, or behind, someone who is complaining into her cell phone. If you aren't yet clear on what makes *you* batty—as well as how to immediately deal with your triggers so you don't spend more time than you need to in a state of agitation—then it's time to both pinpoint your stressors and come up with an in-the-moment irritation buster.

You cannot get rid of things that annoy you, but you can learn not to be stressed (or to be less stressed) by them.

"Wisely and slow. They stumble that run fast."
—William Shakespeare

Here are three tools to help you be less affected by anxiety-invoking people, activities, thoughts, and anything else that threatens your inner peace.

Get enough sleep. Studies have shown that people tend to feel more reactive when they are sleep-deprived. If you don't believe you're one of these people, I invite you to try an experiment: get eight hours of sleep every night for a week. Is it easier to stay emotionally even-keeled?

Never say yes right away. You can get overwhelmed when you feel like you need to say yes to everything, from organizing the church bake sale to handing out flyers for the school play. Being overcommitted can fill your days with activities that take you away from your children, your spouse, and your work, and make it impossible to involve yourself in things you actually enjoy. One way to avoid feeling overwhelmed is to say no immediately to things you don't really want to do. Be aware that you will meet with persistent people who push you to commit to something. If you don't feel comfortable saying no right away, then try this script: "That sounds interesting. I can't give you an answer until I consult my calendar, my spouse's calendar, and each of my kid's calendars. Let me do that and I will email you an answer by tomorrow night." This script instantly provides distance between you and a pushy person.

Exercise daily. Depending on which research study you look at, 20 minutes to an hour of moderate exercise can aid lower blood pressure and keep the nervous system running efficiently, helping you maintain your cool the whole day long. Further, when you exercise, your brain releases relaxing, feel-good endorphins, including serotonin and dopamine, which give us a feel of happiness and calm. And exercise helps reduce the risks of heart disease, cancer, and other illnesses.

"Nothing can bring you peace but yourself."
—Ralph Waldo Emerson

10 ON-THE-SPOT TENSION TAMERS

Learning how to be (and stay) calm is important if you want to enjoy the tranquil Danish concept of hygge. If, however, you find it all too easy to slip into anxiety or annoyance, these peace-rendering tools can help pull you back to a centered place.

Take a walk. A short stroll is a useful technique for mitigating stress. Research has found that exercise, including walking, activates special nerve cells in the brain that relax the senses.

Look out a window or gaze at a fish tank for five minutes. Taking a break from office work, household chores, or even a screen with fast-moving images is a powerful way to slow down and get calm. By letting your gaze wander out a window or rest upon fish, your mind empties, your heart rate reduces, and your breathing grows deep and slow. In short, you give yourself a vacation from whatever it is that was causing you stress.

Sniff lavender. The aroma of lavender oil has been found to slow the activity of the nervous system, improve sleep quality, promote relaxation, lift the mood, and reduce anxiety. In Germany, lavender flowers are used as a tea for insomnia, restlessness, and nervous stomach irritations.

Sniff vanilla. The vanilla bean's aroma is scientifically proven to elevate feelings of joy and relaxation.

Happiness is a warm puppy. Want to get centered quickly? Cuddle a puppy, kitten, bunny, or other beloved pet. Research has found that the human brain releases relaxing dopamine and serotonin in the presence of a pet. In studies of dog owners, individuals who owned pooches were less likely to suffer from depression than those without pets. Further, dog owners have lower blood pressure in stressful situations than those without pets. One study even found that when people with borderline hypertension adopted dogs from a shelter, their blood pressure declined significantly within five months. (See the bibliography for details of these studies.)

Listen to waves. Many anxiety-prone people benefit from CDs or apps that play the sound of ocean waves. And for a good reason: the sound of waves is incredibly relaxing. Research has found that calming sounds block out other noises that the brain may interpret as threats, thus creating a deep sense of well-being.

Or listen to rain. Or a babbling brook. These sounds work just as well as calming background noises as the crash of ocean waves.

Play Mozart (or another favorite classical composer). A 2007 study of postoperative patients published in *Critical Care Medicine* found that those who listened to sonatas by Mozart showed a reduced need for pain medication, lower blood pressure, and lower levels of stress hormones.

Stretch. A quick stretch, done any time you feel stressed, can leave you feeling at ease. This makes sense when you consider that stress can restrict blood flow to the brain and body (including muscles). When blood flow is reduced, we're left feeling foggy, irritable, and cramped. Stretching improves circulation to the brain and body, allowing us to feel relaxed and comfortable.

Smile. The "feel-good" neurotransmitters dopamine, endorphins, and serotonin are all released when we smile, helping to relieve stress and lower blood pressure. If this sounds overly simplistic, studies have shown the validity of smiling away stress.

Coziness begins with how you feel, something you have a large amount of control over. Do what you can to give yourself the gift of calm and you'll be able to create hygge wherever you go.

CHAPTER THREE

COZY SPACES: CLEARING OUT THE CLUTTER

Danes are a grateful people. Because they tend to be thankful for what they have, they don't feel the need to amass more. This is at the core of hygge: enjoy what you have. At the opposite end of the spectrum is stuffing our homes with stockpiles of items.

Clutter isn't cozy—in Denmark, the United States, or anywhere! Perhaps you have a pile of clothing catalogs strewn on the dining room table, or a dozen bottles of hair-care products crowded onto a small bathtub ledge. Or maybe there are always two or three stacks of folded laundry that you move between your bed and a chair because putting them in your kids' clothing drawers takes too much work. Or your kids' homework and artwork has made your fridge look more like an over-grown bulletin board than a kitchen appliance.

The first key to dealing with clutter is to identify it. When you relax in your space, do you notice the unorganized stack of music sitting on the piano bench? Or the colored pencils under the dining room table? Or the dishes in the dish drainer? If you notice them, they're clutter.

We each have a different relationship with tidiness and organization, which means something that doesn't even catch my eye may be clutter to yours. Does your space feel cluttered *to you*? If you answered no, then move on to the next chapter. If you answered something along the lines of maybe, sometimes, often, or yes, then let's dig in and rein in our clutter.

HOW CLUTTER CAN AFFECT YOU

A comfort-driven life doesn't have room for clutter. Here are the many benefits of keeping your space tidy.

Clutter affects your ability to focus. Researchers at the Princeton Neuroscience Institute used functional magnetic resonance imaging and other psychological tools to map the brain's response to organized and disorganized stimuli and to monitor task performance. They found that being exposed to clutter affected test subjects' ability to process information as effectively as possible.

Clutter can make you feel depressed and more. From 2001 to 2005 researchers from UCLA's Center on Everyday Lives of Families explored the relationship between 32 California families and clutter. Among the findings was a link between high density of household objects and high cortisol (the stress hormone) levels in female homeowners. The more stuff, the more stress women feel. (Men, on the other hand, didn't find mess as off-putting.)

The clutter–obesity connection. Researchers from Cornell University studied 101 women and found that those who eat in a cluttered kitchen consume 103 more calories per sitting than individuals who eat in an organized kitchen. The study was published the journal *Environment and Behavior* in 2016.

Clutter can negatively affect many areas of your life. A 2016 study titled "Stuff Happens," undertaken by the Australia Institute, surveyed 1,000 Australians about clutter. The findings show that 88 percent of homes have at least one cluttered room; 4 in 10 Australians say they feel anxious, guilty, or depressed about clutter in their homes; and the average Australian spends $1,226 a year on items that have been purchased and never used. And 59 percent of women said there was a room in the house that they didn't like visitors to see because of clutter.

Clutter can be embarrassing. In the 2016 Australian survey mentioned above, 32 percent of female respondents agreed that clutter made them feel embarrassed; 17 percent worried their children would inherit their clutter, and 20 percent agreed that clutter caused conflict with a partner or family member.

People who are at risk of becoming hoarders have poor sleep. Research conducted by the American Academy of Sleep Medicine in 2015 found that those participants at risk of hoarding disorder scored significantly higher for sleep abnormalities—including trouble falling asleep, trouble staying asleep, and daytime sleepiness—on sleep surveys.

CLUTTER VS. HOARDING

Merriam Webster's definition of clutter is one you probably know: *disordered things that impede movement or reduce effectiveness*. In real-life verbiage, clutter is the stack of mail and homework scattered on the hall table, the magazines lying on the floor near the bed, the makeup and skin-care pots perched on the bathroom counter, or the toys littering the family room floor. It is unsightly and pulls attention from living. But for the most part, clutter is a temporary situation, just waiting to be cleaned up and turned into order. Clutter is what happens when we don't have a system for organizing things, or when we bring things into our home without first getting rid of items to make room for the newcomers.

Hoarding, however, is a more permanent and severe state of being, which shows up as gargantuan stacks, piles, and mounds of items that make moving around in a home almost impossible. Thought to affect up to 6 percent of the population, hoarding disorder manifests itself in difficulty discarding items the rest of the world would see as trash, often flyers, magazines, newspapers, packing material, bulk-bought groceries, or cleaning supplies. These items accumulate in the home, limiting activities and putting people at risk of fires, falling, poor sanitation, loneliness, depression, lowered immune system function, and other health concerns. If you or someone you know suffers from hoarding, seek medical attention.

IT'S NOT JUST ABOUT CLUTTER: DIRT MATTERS

A home can be so organized and tidy that not even a loose pencil or a tilted family photo can be found, but still have a layer of dust on the piano, grime on the windows, and sticky spots on the kitchen floor. Clutter and dirt are two different things. And they both need to be tackled to make a house a cozy home.

If someone unexpectedly dropped by your home right now, would you be comfortable inviting that person in? If you feel you need to quickly run the vacuum or wipe down your entryway walls and floor while pretending you cannot hear the doorbell, then your home is dirtier than is comfortable for you. When you relax in your space, do you notice the dust bunnies under the sofa? The fingerprints on the bathroom door? Or the coffee stain on the counter? If you notice them, they're a problem.

Every family has a different system for regular cleaning, though Danes tend to spot clean a bit each weekday evening, and do an

in-depth housecleaning once a week, when the entire family tidies up the home. In my own childhood, Saturday morning was the regrettable time earmarked for deep cleaning. While my friends were outside skating and playing ball, my mother expected me to vacuum both floors of our two-story home, dust the lower level, and do the dishes—before handing me over to my dad, who would typically order me to weed the family food garden and maybe help him change the oil in his car. If I was lucky, I would be done by 10 a.m. and have enough time to watch cartoons and run around with neighbors before coming in for lunch.

Today I do things differently. Each evening, from 8 to 8:30, I do as much as I can within that 30 minutes. For me, this is usually folding laundry, vacuuming, cleaning up the two bathrooms, and maybe dusting. When the half hour is over, I am done; anything not finished gets tackled the next day.

HOW TO PUT YOUR HOUSEKEEPING ON AUTOMATIC PILOT

Housekeeping is my word for both decluttering and cleaning. The easiest way to make housekeeping an automatic part of your life is to make it a habit. If that sounds overly simplistic to you, I'm glad. It really is uncomplicated. Make housekeeping a habit and you'll have a calm, cozy, clean, tidy home—a warm, inviting space that you feel comfortable sharing with others. This is hygge, and all it takes to create it is practice. The following ideas may help.

Address your dirt and clutter hot spots daily. You may not have the desire to clean your entire house each day, but if your dining room table gets lost each afternoon under a fresh pile of kids' homework, backpacks, and junk mail, clear it off each evening. If you have a cat and litter from the box is scattered all over the bathroom floor, sweep it up each night. And so on. Letting hot spots go for more than a day means chaos and extra work for you.

Pay for help if you want to. Hiring help is often a worthwhile investment for those who can pull it off. Pay someone to come in once a week, every two weeks, or once a month. Request a ceiling-to-floorboard scrubbing or hand over just the tasks you loathe or aren't physically up to doing and perform the easier jobs yourself.

Everyone should help. Everyone who lives in a space has an obligation to help keep it clean. Be brave and have a frank discussion with your family or roommates about how often cleaning should take place and how in-depth it should be.

Children must help keep their space clean and tidy. I am always amused when I hear people complain about "children these days." They don't have the work ethic that we did as kids, they don't know how to do anything around the home, they're oblivious to dirt, and so on. But these same grumblers do not require their children to help keep their homes orderly. How are children ever to develop competence and homemaking skills if they aren't given the chance to learn them? Today's children are very busy—perhaps busier than we were as kids. I have gone through periods where I have let my sons off the housework hook due to their daily workloads. But when I realized that one of my kids, at 13, didn't know how to operate a vacuum, I toughened up. Every single night, from 8:00 to 8:30, my kids help clean. They know how to wash walls, clean a toilet, dust, and fold clothes. And having the help each evening allows me to spend less of my own time on cleaning.

Choose your best day. Many people I know were forced to clean on Saturdays or Sundays when their neighborhood friends were outdoors playing. With today's schedules, however, weekends are often some of our busiest days—not the best time for piling on more activities (even something as important as cleaning). Experiment with weekday cleaning. Tuesdays, Wednesdays, and Thursdays work especially well for many people, as they are often less harried than Mondays and less busy than weekends.

Once a week or once a day? Most homes need a moderately deep room-by-room cleaning at least once a week. By this I mean a quick decluttering, vacuuming, dusting, and wiping down any grimy surfaces. If, however, you don't have a large chunk of weekly time to devote to cleaning, opt for doing a bit each day. Cleaning for 30 minutes each evening works for us.

Make cleaning fun—or at least more fun. Do whatever it takes to make the process less painful. I have been known to bribe my kids and myself with snacks, contests, fragrant cleaning products, and anything else I can think of to make cleaning more enjoyable.

Do one deep clean each month. My daily clean is what I like to call a "just below the surface clean." Everything is picked up and degermed, degreased, and swept clean of dust, dog hair, and fingerprints. Once a month, however, I like to go deep and clean the windows, shampoo the rugs, clean the sofa, wipe down the shelves of the medicine cabinet, make the inside of the fridge sparkle, descuff the baseboards, wax the floors, reorganize the pantry shelves, and so forth. I put this on the calendar and send everyone in the home an invitation for that day. If you don't have a household of possible help, consider hiring a cleaning service to come in once a month for a deep clean. It is money well spent.

Do one small load of laundry each evening. If you have an in-home washer and dryer, gather up the clothing and towels from the day and do a load of wash on the quickest setting.

Don't bring junk mail into the house. At all. Anything those letters and postcards contain—including promo codes or special "secret" sales info—can be found online. Trust me.

HOMEMADE CLEANING PRODUCTS

Traditionally, natural ingredients—such as vegetable and nut oils, culinary acids (like lemon juice and vinegar), and baking soda—were used by people all over the world to polish wood and clean and shine metal, leather, and upholstery. Denmark is no different. And in fact, many Danes continue, even today, to use cleaning products based on natural ingredients. It may not surprise you to hear that Danes don't keep a lot of cleaning products around—not because they don't clean but because they often opt for homemade cleaning products like the ones that follow.

DISPOSABLE CLEANING WIPES
FOR GENERAL CLEANING

Some people love the convenience of premoistened wipes, and these house-cleaning wipes are great for cleaning countertops and other kitchen and bathroom surfaces. I use them to spot wash doors and walls before guests arrive (that's when I tend to notice fingerprints most clearly), as well as for wiping down dirty toy bins, appliances, pencil cases, rain boots, and more.

MAKES 20

20 heavy-duty dinner napkins or sturdy, thick paper towels

1 cup slightly warmed distilled water in a liquid measuring cup (using a 2-cup size or larger measuring cup makes this recipe easier)

1 tablespoon coconut oil

5 drops of your favorite essential oil or blend of oils

1. Stack the napkins or paper towels in a deep rectangular baking pan or food storage container.

2. Into the warmed distilled water, pour the coconut oil and add the essential oil. Stir well.

3. Slowly pour half of the mixture around the sides of the napkins and the rest on the top of the napkins.

4. Cover the pan with plastic wrap (or cover the container with its lid) and let your wipes sit and soak up the liquid for 1 hour.

5. Remove and place into a clean, reusable baby wipe container or food storage container.

HOMEMADE GLASS CLEANER

I keep several spray bottles of this in the house (one in the kitchen and one in each bathroom) at all times.

MAKES 2¹/₂ CUPS

¹/₄ cup white vinegar

1 teaspoon liquid dish detergent or liquid castile soap

2 cups water

Optional: 5 drops of your favorite essential oil

Combine all ingredients in a clean, empty spray bottle. Shake before using.

HARDWOOD FLOOR CLEANER

This coconut oil–based floor cleaner leaves wood floors absolutely lustrous—and it's economical and simple to make and use. This recipe makes enough to clean a 2,000-square-foot house. You'll need to make up a new batch each time you mop. (I also use this on our piano.)

MAKES 2³/₄ CUPS

2 cups white or apple cider vinegar

¹/₂ cup lemon juice

¹/₄ cup liquid coconut oil

20 drops of your favorite essential oil (or use a mix of your favorites)

1. In a large bowl or jar, stir or shake together all ingredients.

2. Pour the mixture into a 2-gallon bucket.

3. Add hot water to the bucket until the bucket is about two-thirds full.

4. Apply to the floor with a sponge mop. No rinsing required.

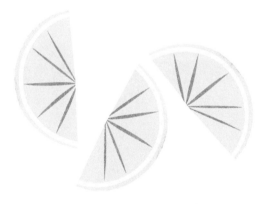

TILE AND LINOLEUM CLEANER

This cleaner is great for bathroom and kitchen tile—any tile, really! Make a new batch each time you clean.

3 cups white vinegar

2 tablespoons liquid dish detergent or liquid castile soap

$^1/_2$ tablespoon coconut oil

10 drops of your favorite essential oil

1. In a large bowl or jar, stir or shake together all ingredients.

2. Pour the mixture into a 2-gallon bucket.

3. Add hot water to the bucket until about two-thirds full.

4. Apply to the floor with a sponge mop. No rinsing required.

HOMEMADE TUB, SINK, AND TOILET CLEANER

This is a fun cleaner to make with kids—it foams! The baking soda and vinegar create the bubbles. (Do you remember that volcano experiment in elementary school science class?) This makes enough for cleaning one bathroom.

MAKES 1²/₃ CUPS

1 cup baking soda

¹/₄ cup white vinegar

¹/₃ cup liquid castile soap

1 tablespoon liquid coconut oil

2 tablespoons coarse kosher salt

20 drops of your favorite essential oil or blend of essential oils

1. Add the baking soda to a 2-gallon bucket. Slowly add the vinegar. It will foam up as it reacts—be ready for it!

2. Add the remaining ingredients to bucket and mix with a wooden spoon.

3. To use as a toilet bowl cleaner, pour ¹/₄ cup of the solution into the toilet before scrubbing.

4. To use as a cleaner for the exterior of your toilet, for your sink, or your tub, decant the solution into a spray bottle. Spray the cleanser directly onto the surface and allow it to sit for 5 minutes before scrubbing the surface with a damp scrub brush or wiping down with a sponge. Repeat as necessary.

WALL WASH

My sons and husband are terrible with our walls. Chalk and crayon, pencil, fingerprints, grease, tomato sauce, nut butter, coffee splatters...my walls see a lot of action. My kids use this cleanser to clean the walls as one of their weekly chores.

MAKES MORE THAN 1 QUART

1 quart warm water

¼ cup white vinegar

2 tablespoons biodegradable liquid soap

Sponges or soft cloths

1. Mix all ingredients in a 1- or 2-gallon bucket.
2. Soak a sponge or soft cloth with cleanser and rub onto walls.
3. Repeat as necessary.

HOW TO RESIST THE PULL OF STUFF

Most of us love to acquire new things. But if you are trying to live a calm, centered life in a warm, inviting, cozy home—which is what hygge is all about—it's important to resist the pull of more things. As one of my Danish friends says, "The more things you crowd into your life, the less life you have room for in your life." Fortunately, there are ways to short-circuit that inborn urge to stockpile more stuff. Here are some simple tools.

Have a goal you are working toward. Spending money on an experience, an education, or paying off debt is a wonderful way to honor yourself. Next time you find yourself pining for a new sofa or shoes, ask yourself if they will feel as good as repaying your student loan or surprising your parents with a family trip to Jamaica. As a gift to yourself, apply the price of the resisted item toward your goal.

Wait a month. Whatever it is you want to bring home—from a pair of pumps to a new duvet—give yourself a month to think about it. If you still want the item after a month, then go for it.

Nothing new comes in before two old things go out. In our home, whenever we bring in an item—be it a shirt or a coffee mug—two things must leave. This makes us think about how much we want something before we commit to owning it.

Ignore sales, coupons, promo codes, and the like. Sales and other markdowns benefit the companies you buy from. All they really do for you is allow you to add more clutter to your life for less money. Not buying something will always be the most cost-effective and clutter-busting choice—promo code or no promo code.

Do not read catalogs or sale circulars. The more you look at things you do not have, the more you will want them. Remove temptation and you'll be less likely to find yourself purchasing items you do not

need—and less likely to hear your partner or kids asking for things they do not need.

What is in your space—as well as what is not in your space—affects your mood and influences how you feel about your home. The simple act of tidying up plays a huge role in creating an atmosphere of comfort and warmth. This is the gift of hygge. Enjoy it!

CHAPTER FOUR

COZY HOMES: WARMTH IS ALL AROUND YOU

Is there a cozier word than *home*? A home is so much more than a shelter or a residence. It is the most comfortable place on Earth, a sanctuary where you can relax and be yourself, with no judgments. Home is a restorative, reassuring place to return to each evening after being out in the frantic, harsh world, or a safe harbor of sorts that you revisit each year—as if on a pilgrimage—to sink into the warmth of family bonds and reconnect to those people, places, and memories that shaped your childhood.

Home is a hook to anchor a conversation, and perhaps a blossoming friendship. It is also a hook on which we hang memories. The places we have lived help organize recollections of our past. In exploring, being in, and bumping up against these places, we have been shaped into the people we are now.

Having a home base that supports you and nourishes your spirit will change your life. This isn't hyperbole. This idea of home as a safe haven is at the heart of coziness. And this brings us to hygge and how to invite it into our homes.

WHERE TO BEGIN

While creating a cozy home doesn't happen overnight, you'll be happy to learn that it is not an intensive, complicated process. Nor is it expensive. With a few simple actions, you'll notice that your home suddenly feels fresher, lighter, warmer, and more inviting. Here are some easy foundational steps that you can take right now to cozy up your home.

Read chapter 3 on decluttering your home. Once all the extraneous stuff is gone, light, warmth, and energy can flow unimpeded through your space, giving you a better idea of what more you can do to create a sense of hygge.

Don't tolerate bad odors. Invest in or make a room deodorizing spray, or, if no one has sensitivities, get naturally scented candles. Humans have hundreds of odor receptor genes, which help us distinguish pleasurable odors from dangerous ones. Musty, musky, dirty smells make us uncomfortable and create a distracting atmosphere. I always receive compliments from people on how nice my house smells—my secret is keeping my kitchen and bathrooms clean and using naturally scented candles. A pleasant-smelling house is one people (the home's owners included) love to be in.

Let there be light. Change your light bulbs and add lighting where needed. Darkness in small doses can be romantic and moody—but if your house is darker than the midday light on a clear September day, it is too dark. Living in a dark home can make you prone to depression, distraction, sadness, fatigue, and so on. Easy tricks you can use to bring more light into your home include using brighter bulbs in your existing light fixtures, installing more light fixtures or lamps, and keeping window coverings open during the day. Adding mirrors to rooms to reflect light can also give your home a warm, sunny feeling.

Music creates moods. Invest in CDs or make a playlist of uplifting music that makes you feel calm and happy. Music has been found to manipulate moods—it can speed up your heart rate and create feelings of anger or aggression, or help to slow your heart rate and leaving you feeling relaxed and safe. Much of this has to do with the music's tempo, the volume of its drums and bass, and whether it uses smooth legato tones or choppy staccato notes. Classical music (by composers such as Mozart, Haydn, and Beethoven) and baroque music (by composers such as Vivaldi, Bach, and Handel) are especially effective at evoking a sense of happiness and calm.

Do something about all those cords and chargers. Nothing clutters the look of a room like a tangle of cords and power strips. Run cords through the wall, use a cord management system, or mount power strips to the underside of bookshelves, side tables, cabinetry, and sofas.

"There is nothing like staying at home
for real comfort."

—Jane Austen

Get rid of your throw pillows. Danes don't use throw pillows, which they see as visual clutter. Americans, however, seem to love them. My father always used to joke about all the throw pillows my mother placed on the sofas and beds in our family home. My mom saw these pillows as beautiful works of art, made by talented friends. But as stunning as these pillows were, they gave rooms an untidy, overly fussy look. Plus, they were a constant source of annoyance, having to be moved so people could sit (or sleep) on the furniture underneath these pillows. If you are a pillow lover who cannot imagine living without your collection, here is a challenge: put the pillows away for a month and see how your room feels. I suspect it will feel larger, cleaner, and more energy filled.

Buy a candle for every room. Danes are crazy for candles. In fact, candles are the unofficial symbol of the hygge movement. Like most things Scandinavian, there's a practical reason candles are so important: during the long, dimly lit, cold northern winters, candles are how Danes bring light and warmth to their indoor winter lives. For most Scandinavians, a lit candle creates an instant connection to the warmth of their childhood. To avoid creating indoor air pollution, choose natural, vegetable-based or beeswax candles that are unscented or scented with a favorite essential oil. Be sure to place candles in a safe, stable spot, where they won't be knocked over by a child or a pet and where the flame is far from paper, cloth, or anything else flammable.

Add a vase of flowers or a plant. Bringing plants indoors is an easy way to infuse your environment with oxygen while simultaneously cleansing the air of impurities. Being near plants has other benefits for humans, as well. Cut flowers and living plants create a feeling of calm and beautify rooms. Scientific studies have found that flowers create feelings of joy in those who receive them. Why not harness that lovely feeling and display flowers throughout your home? If real flowers and live plants are too much upkeep for you, invest in high-quality faux flowers and plants for a few of your rooms. Just make sure a few of your rooms boast the real thing.

Get rid of the grays. As popular as gray is in some interior decorating circles, it has a reputation as being a cold, unemotional, and even depressing color. It's not the kind of color that creates a warm, inviting, light-filled space. Science supports this. Researchers at University Hospital of South Manchester in the UK asked 323 people to describe their moods using a color. Thirty percent of people with anxiety chose gray to describe their state, while more than 50 percent of depressed respondents chose gray.

Paint your walls light yellow. In the above study, guess which color happy people most often used to describe their mood? You guessed it: yellow! In Denmark, pale yellow walls are a favorite way to bring warmth, happiness, and light to a room. If you can't get excited about warm, pale yellow (as opposed to icy or lemony yellow) walls, then try a warm white. Just make sure the shade has no gray undertones.

Limit colors to two or three. Color adds a gorgeous pop of excitement to your rooms. But too much color in a room can be distracting rather than cozy or calming. Find a great neutral color—such as beige, tan, off-white, or pale yellow—and accent it with one or two muted or bright shades.

Use art wisely. Art is in the eye of the beholder, meaning anything from a twisted log of driftwood to a barbed wire sculpture can be art. If your goal is to infuse your home with a welcoming atmosphere of warmth, light, and comfort, how you decorate your home matters. Art—no matter how skillful or brilliant—that portrays violence, which leaves the viewer feeling disturbed, or is made of jagged or sharp angles belongs at a museum or an art gallery. For a cozy home, choose uplifting, comforting art, be that landscapes, photographs of family members, children's sculptures, or anything else that makes one feel good. Be careful, however, not to go overboard. Less art is definitely more: too many things on the wall or too many items on shelves creates a cluttered look rather than a peaceful vibe.

Choose furniture in the same color. Walk into a living room with a green sofa, a maple wood end table, a black chair, a blond wood coffee table, and a tan loveseat. What do you have? Visual overload. Limiting furniture colors is an important and easy way to create a warm, comfortable visual landscape.

Get some rugs. Plush rugs invite people into a room, encouraging them to take off their shoes and stay awhile. In Denmark, it's common for people to hang out on the floor, making rugs an especially thoughtful way to create a comfortable environment. Just make sure your rugs match your room's color scheme—otherwise, the room will look cluttered and uninviting.

Remove obstacles. Move anything that is blocking a door, hallway, window, or room, or that is making it hard to move about your home easily. In feng shui—the ancient Chinese system of balancing harmonies in an environment—it is important that energy be able to move unencumbered through and around rooms. So it is, also, with hygge. Anything—from furniture to a backpack left on a hallway floor—that bars free movement in a home should be removed. Barriers of any kind (even when unintentional) create a cramped, uncozy feeling.

In addition to the above hygge-creating tips, there are targeted steps you can take within specific rooms to increase your home's cozy quotient. Here's a room-by-room rundown.

HALLWAYS

In feng shui, the front hallway is one of the most critical points of the home—as the entryway into the home's inner sanctum, it must allow positive energy to flow easily inside and is the first thing a visitor sees. With hygge, the entryway serves the same purpose. Therefore, it should be devoid of clutter, painted in a light color, and have clean walls and floors. This goes for all of a home's hallways. Make sure yours are well lit, with attractive ceiling fixtures—many people spend energy choosing perfect lighting fixtures for their living rooms and bathrooms, only to forget their hallways. Other tips:

- Many hallways have chipped baseboards or floorboards or peeling paint around doors. If this sounds familiar, spend a couple hours making repairs.

- Avoid overdecorating hallways. Two facing walls lined with photographs can create a cluttered effect. Limit art to one side of the hallway, leaving the other wall clean.

- Do not use runners or rugs in your hallways. These collect dirt, are a safety hazard, and make hallways look cramped and crowded. Bare floors are safest and easiest to keep clean.

- Hanging coat pegs near a door is fine, as long as the hallway is a wide one. Coats and backpacks hung in a narrow corridor will be constantly knocked down as people squeeze by.

LIVING AND FAMILY ROOMS

In Western architecture, a living room, also called a lounge or sitting room, is a room in a residential house or apartment for relaxing and socializing. When I was growing up, we had both a family room, where the family hung out on bean bags and watched television together, and a living room, where my parents entertained visitors and where we children were not allowed. Regardless of which you have, this important room is often the centerpiece of a home.

As a heavily used common room, your living room must be both comfortable and well kept. Here are a few ways you can meet this challenge.

- Don't overdecorate. Decorating for decorating's sake causes clutter. Get rid of the vacation souvenirs on the bookshelves, the various books that no one has read stacked on your end tables, and so on.

- Now, get rid of a few more things. This room has more bodies in it at one time than any other room in your home. That alone will create a bit of clutter. If there is anything you can clear out, do it.

- Opt for sleek. Heavy, ornate furniture can look untidy in such a busy room. A sleek sofa or two with a few clean-lined chairs and maybe a bean bag (plus a rug to lounge on) give a larger number of people comfortable, neat-looking places to plant themselves while they enjoy one another's company.

- Get the lighting off the furniture. Instead of standing and table lamps, opt for wall- and ceiling-mounted lighting. This creates an organized, neat look and makes it less likely something will get knocked over.

- Be daring and go screen-free—no television screens, visible computers, or laptops lying about. Discretely position a music station somewhere and see what your family and friends come up with when they don't have a screen to stare at. If you must have a screen, consider mounting one with a cover or placing it behind a cabinet door, so it isn't immediately visible to guests.

- Place any instruments you play in the living room. A piano, standing organ, or guitar is a recipe for fun. Kids love sitting down and plunking out melodies.

- To encourage group fun, keep a stack of board games or other group activities in a prominent place on a coffee table or shelf.

KITCHEN AND PANTRY

The kitchen can be one of the messiest, dirtiest rooms in the home. This is not a comfortable thought when you consider the connection between tidiness and sanitation. Fortunately, there are easy things you can try to keep your food center calm and tidy.

- Read chapter 6 for ideas regarding cooking, storing food, and outfitting a kitchen.

- When cleaning your kitchen each day, don't forget to check the ceiling, cabinets, appliances, vents, and floor. So many of us spend time wiping down countertops but forget the grease and grime that build up in other areas.

- Keep your sink smelling fresh by cleaning it each night before bed and sprinkling a tablespoon of baking soda in the drain to neutralize food odors.

- Take out your garbage daily. In an attempt to avoid dealing daily with garbage, many people install huge trash cans that can hold a week's worth of waste. Allowing garbage to sit in your home runs counter to the clean, calm living space you are trying to create. Get a smaller trash can and empty it daily. Buy compostable bags and compost material if you can. Take the recycling out each night. Get in the habit of moving refuse out of your home regularly. If you want to install large garbage bins in the garage or yard, fine. Just don't allow garbage to build up in the home.

- Make sure your kitchen is light and bright. You want your time in this important room to be enjoyable—so enjoyable that people come to join you. Use bright bulbs and add extra overhead or wall-mounted lighting. Light not only makes cooking and eating more pleasant but also helps with kitchen inventory, revealing items lurking in the back of shelves and cupboards.

- Discard chipped, cracked, bent, or otherwise broken serving pieces and dinnerware. Even if the item is still usable, drinking out of a cup with a crack or eating off a chipped plate does not feel good.

- Make sure your kitchen has good air flow. Many apartment kitchens, for instance, do not include ventilation. In some places, kitchens are squeezed into odd, dank corners of the home. If your kitchen does not have an adequate flow of fresh air, install a ceiling fan or mount an oscillating fan in a corner of the room.

- Keep televisions and screens out of your kitchen. In an effort to live in a more hygge manner, preparation and enjoyment of food should be done without distraction. Watching a talk show, ordering items online, and texting friends are all wonderful when done singularly—but they should not be performed while cooking or eating.

- Do not use your kitchen as a repository for bills, junk mail, flyers, or the like. Paper is one of the biggest room-cluttering agents of the modern era, giving rooms a slovenly, chaotic look. If you don't put a bill on your kitchen counter, you won't have to move it from your kitchen.

"There is no sincerer love than the love of food."

—George Bernard Shaw

DINING ROOM

While some apartments and smaller homes having dining areas attached to their kitchens, most American homes have a separate dining room that is located just off the kitchen. Some families use their dining rooms daily. Others eat at the kitchen counter most days and use the dining room for holidays, dinner parties, and other special occasions. Whichever of these best describes your situation, the dining room holds a special place in a home. Here are some easy ways to give it the respect it deserves.

° Use your dining room regularly. Kitchen counters are convenient, but there is something about sitting down at a dining room table that says "special meal." This goes for solo meals or group dining—eating in your dining room creates an air of reverence and celebration.

° Do not use your dining room table as a station for mail, backpacks, craft supplies, or other items. The dining room will feel coziest and most comfortable if your table is left clean and clear of items. If you'd like, drape a tablecloth over the table and place a centerpiece on it.

° Do not use your dining room as a storage closet. When I was growing up, I loved my Danish grandparents' dining room: it was light, clean, and uncluttered and was used for every meal. My American grandparents' dining room, however, was another story. Not only did it contain a large table, but lining the walls were a piano, an office desk, a china cabinet, and extra dishes and chairs that didn't "fit" in any other part of the home. The room felt so cramped that it was rarely used; everyone preferred to eat in their bright kitchen instead.

- There should be ample space to walk around the dining room table when the chairs are occupied. If there is not, purchase a smaller table. You need to be able to move around your dining room, even if that means choosing a small four-person table and chairs.

- If there is not enough room for a sideboard and a china cabinet—two common pieces of dining room furniture—mount high shelves and shallow cabinets for your dinnerware and whatever other items you want to keep in your dining room.

- There should never be a computer, television, game console, or any other type of screen in a dining room.

- If you do not use your dining room frequently, you may not see the need to vacuum, dust, and clean in there regularly. Dust and dirt build up whether you use a room or not. Clean your dining room when you clean the rest of your home.

BATHROOM

Ah, the bathroom—another one of the untidiest rooms in the home. If you've ever shared a bathroom with a teenager or with a cosmetics hoarder, you know how cluttered and unclean this room can be. Fortunately, there are things you can do to make this room cozy and comfortable.

- Make sure your bathroom has enough light. Change the bulbs and install ceiling- and wall-mounted lights if needed. A dark bathroom not only feels claustrophobic, it encourages mold and fungus growth.

- Get rid of gray and gray-like colors. This means no taupe, mauve, lavender, maroon or wine, deep blue or black, or gray of any shade. Bathrooms should feature bright, clear, light-creating colors. Opt for warm whites and beiges, with accents of welcoming green, yellow, pink, turquoise, pale orange, coral, or another cozy color.

- Check the air quality. Some bathrooms are interior rooms with no vents or windows. Hang a small ceiling- or wall-mounted fan to keep air moving.

- Keep your toilet, bathroom counter, shower curtain, tub, sink, and tiles clean. A quick wipe-down each morning takes minutes and will deliver a welcoming, clean space that does not embarrass you.

- How does your bathroom smell? Does your bathroom smell like mold or other stinky things? If so, getting a fan and using more light (to prevent the growth of odor-creating mold and fungus, both of which prefer darkness) will help, but also add a few candles or an aromatherapy infuser. These are safer for your lungs and the environment than relying on random blasts of aerosol room fragrance.

- Check for mildew. Mold and mildew in the grout, shower door or curtain, or tub looks and smells bad. Regularly clean away mildew. If an item is so infused with the stuff that you can't get it clean, replace it with a new one.

- Choose decorations wisely. The bathroom is a humid place—not great for photos and paintings. Opt for low-light plants or mirrors and skip the baskets of shells and rocks that many people sit on their toilet tanks. They clutter the room, making it look even smaller than it may already be. Pretty towels and bath mats are an easy, practical way to decorate the room.

BEDROOMS AND GUEST BEDROOMS

Bedrooms are sanctuaries—places where we go to shake off the annoyances of the day. They are also deeply personal places that are often decorated to show off the interests or accolades of their owners. Here are some tips to keep your bedroom from becoming cluttered and overly fussy.

- While bedrooms are used primarily for sleeping, it's important that they not be too dark. A dark bedroom can leave you in a dark mood, as human moods often mirror their surroundings. Instead of relying on a lamp on a bedside table, consider installing ceiling-mounted lights or hanging lighting high on one or more of your walls.

- Use warm, inviting colors. You may have heard the old advice to use shades of blue in the bedroom to encourage drowsiness and avoid shades of red and orange, which can create wakefulness. While there is some truth in that, it's important to your home's "hygge quotient" to skip overly cool colors, such as gray, grayed blues, deep blues, and cool purples. These can create a cold, sterile feeling. Opt for sandy tans, mild greens, toasty browns, muted turquoise, pale yellow, and other warm shades.

- Get rid of the screens. Studies have found that having screens (television, computer, game consoles, or phones) in your bedroom increases the risk of disrupted sleep cycles and weight gain, while decreasing the hours you sleep each night and your daytime attention. Several studies have found that children who watch some type of screen at night are heavier than their peers, are more susceptible to underage cigarette and alcohol use, and may experience irritability and attention issues during waking hours.

- Remove visible clutter. Many people use their bedrooms to hide items they don't want seen in more public rooms. However, a cluttered bedroom does not create a feeling of lightness, comfort, and well-being. If you don't have closet or storage space in another area of the home for your stuff, get rid of it. This goes for the guest bedroom as well, which is a room is for the care of guests.

- Do not eat in your bedroom. This was an ironclad rule for my siblings and me when we were growing up. Eating was done at the kitchen, dining room, or backyard picnic table. Sleeping and play took place in bedrooms. Now that I am adult, I am surprised at how many dirtied bowls and plates I see on people's bedside tables or—worse—the floor around their beds. Eating in your bedroom undermines its role as an inner sanctum, a place where you go to rest and recharge. Plus, it is unsightly and can attract pests.

- Choose appropriate art. The images that you see right before slumber affect your state of mind during sleep, which in turn can affect your sleep cycles. No matter how famous the artist or how dazzling the work, avoid pieces that depict suffering, violence, or anything disturbing. Choose uplifting pieces and plants to decorate your special space.

- Do not keep clothing on chairs, exercise equipment, or beds. If you do not have a proper closet for clothing, invest in an armoire or wardrobe that will match your room. Keeping clothing and shoes out creates an untidy, cluttered look.

GARAGE

You may think the state of your garage is no one's business but your own—and you'd be right! But if you are committed to living in a more comfortable, graceful way, you'll want to get your garage in order. After all, a disordered garage makes it hard to live an orderly life. Here are some tips.

- Consider your car. My parents used their garage for our cars and had an extra storage area for rakes, shovels, the lawn mower, and other outdoor stuff. But many of my friends' families used their garages for their stuff and kept their cars in the driveway. Guess whose cars were in better shape?

- Most garages are large enough to store both cars and all those items we use to maintain our outdoor spaces. Dedicate the back area of the garage (the area farthest from the garage doors) to storage and workspace. Build cabinets and shelves and install a long workbench. Using pegs and hooks on this wall makes it easy to keep tools and other items neat.

- Keep the garage clean. Regularly scrub away oil stains, sweep out debris, and tidy up your work area so your garage does not look grimy or in disarray.

- Lighting matters. If your garage is not light enough, install brighter bulbs or mount ceiling lights. A dark garage is dangerous: you can bump into a sharp tool and get hurt, drive your car into something when parking, or even miss seeing a person or animal who could be in this space.

- If you enter the home through a garage door, make sure the door is painted in a welcoming color and cleaned weekly.

- Install a carbon monoxide monitor; avoid using gas grills, electric generators, and other items with engines (such as a pressure washer) inside the garage; and never leave your car running in your garage for longer than absolutely necessary.

STORAGE/TOOL SHED

Not everyone has a structure dedicated to storage, but if you have room for a shed, it can be a handy option for storing things you don't want to put in your garage. Just be sure to:

- Install adequate lighting. A dark shed is an inviting place for spiders to nest or snakes to hibernate. Bright light will ensure you see a critter quickly before you get bitten or stung.

- Keep your shed orderly. Any time you are dealing with tools, orderliness is important. A jumble of trowels, hand shovels, picks, and screwdrivers are a recipe for injury. Make sure there are boxes, cabinets, pegs, and shelves for all items.

- Put a lock on the door. And keep the door locked. This will ensure children don't use the shed as a hiding place or don't borrow something sharp.

PORCHES, BALCONIES, DECKS, AND TERRACES

Porches and other outdoor spaces are incredibly inviting. But if not kept orderly, they give your home a cluttered, rundown look that is visible to anyone who passes by. Maybe you've heard the old saying "How you do one thing is how you do everything." If you have clutter in your outdoor spaces, it will affect the way your indoor spaces feel. For cozy outdoor spaces:

- Keep them free of stuff. A chair or two, a table, a grill—these are perfect deck-worthy items. Boxes of beach toys, a few tricycles, a pogo stick, and an old gerbil cage are not. Toss the junk or find an enclosed storage space for it.

- Keep your balcony or other outdoor space clean. Sweep up the leaves, wipe away bird droppings, bring in the used tumblers and plates, and so on.

- Add plants—a few on the ground and a few hanging from planters. Plants give indoor and outdoor spaces a fresh, comfortable look that puts people at ease.

- If your outdoor furniture does not match, consider covering it in a warm, neutral fabric.

- Repair or replace broken outdoor furniture.

- Keep your balcony or other outdoor space in good repair. You want to feel safe when leaning on a railing or when inviting more than one person up to a deck.

YARDS

One of the greatest joys of my childhood was playing with my neighborhood friends in one of our front or backyards. These private outdoor areas provided a safe, comfortable space to dream, explore, rest, roughhouse, or just sit quietly and watch passersby. Most of the yards in my neighborhood were neat, tidy, and inviting. Some were lined with herbs or flowers, and some were a single expanse of lawn. Others featured trees or shrubbery. One even boasted a vegetable garden. If you are lucky enough to have a yard, here are some ways to make it more inviting.

- Consider safety over privacy. If you have a row of hedges that could be a place for animals or unsavory visitors to hide, consider replacing it with a lower row of flowers or herbs.

- Install outdoor lighting where appropriate, making sure to also illuminate far corners.

- Bring bikes, skates, scooters, balls, and other toys in each evening. Leaving items outdoors can make a home look cluttered.

- Remove dead and dying plants. In feng shui, these are said to bring bad luck. In the world of hygge, they are similarly seen as an uncomfortable comment on your ability to maintain your home. If keeping a lawn is too much work for you, or you simply don't want to, consider other alternatives, such as a rock garden or an English-style flower garden.

HOME OFFICE

If you are an entrepreneur or work in a freelance capacity, you may have a home office. Perhaps you have an entire room dedicated to your work, or you have carved out an office from the corner of your bedroom or living room. Regardless of where your home office is located, here are ideas to help you make it a tranquil space.

- Remove televisions and gaming consoles, as well as anything else that can distract you.

- Keep your desk clean. Different systems work for different people. I like to take five minutes at the end of each day to reorder paper, toss anything I don't need, and dust anything that needs it.

- Make sure your chair feels good. If an ergonomic chair is what you need, get one. If a special old-fashioned wooden swivel chair feels wonderful, then use that. An uncomfortable chair will ensure you won't spend much time working.

- Choose quiet. Use a white noise machine if you need to create a noise buffer from the rest of the home.

- Make sure you have enough light. Use bright bulbs and install ceiling- or wall-mounted lights if needed.

- Decorate sparingly. Posters, wall art, and knickknacks on your desk are distracting visual clutter.

- Do not use shades of gray in your office. In the office, gray and gray-kissed colors create a depressing feeling that can distract you from your projects.

DEN OR LIBRARY

Few homes in Denmark have a den or library. If you, however, are fortunate enough to have one of these rooms, here are some tips for making it an oasis of calm.

- Cut visual clutter. Books are interesting to look at. Shelves and shelves of books are even more interesting. Go easy on the wall art and avoid cluttering shelves, desks, or tables with knickknacks.

- Keep books with spine facing out.

- Repair, replace, or discard books, documents, or other damaged items. Having a room of ripped or stained books is more distracting than calming.

- Dust and vacuum often.

- Make sure the lighting is strong enough to read easily.

- Provide comfortable seating so people can, literally, curl up with a good book.

- Make the room a screen-free space.

"If you have a garden and a library, you have everything you need."

— Marcus Tullius Cicero

LAUNDRY AND MUD ROOM

Many people have washing machines and dryers in a small area near the garage door or near a back bathroom. Having a dedicated area for cleaning clothing is a wonderful luxury. Like the bathroom, it's important to make sure that any area dedicated to cleaning is kept clean itself. Here are some ideas:

- Do not allow clean clothing to hang out in a basket, waiting to be folded. Find time each night to fold clothing and put it away. If you, yourself, don't have time for this, assign the task to one of your children or to your partner. You wash and dry the clothes; they fold and put the clothing away.

- Keep laundry soap and other supplies on a shelf or in cabinet. Leaving these out on top of the washer or dryer looks messy.

- Keep the machines and laundry room walls clean.

- Make sure you have enough lighting to easily see any stains or spots on clothing.

CLOSETS

Closet space is a wonderful thing. When I was nineteen, I lived in a West Village apartment in New York for a summer. It was one of those apartments that don't exist anymore: the sixth floor of a walkup, a shared bathroom in the hallway, a bathtub in the kitchen, and not a single closet. You learn a lot about life when you don't have a closet! One of these things is that you need a whole lot less than you think you do. The other is that closet space does not need to be plentiful to be effective.

Here are some ideas for making the most of your closet space, based on the principles of hygge.

- Closets should be organized. No one should ever open a closet door and be faced with an avalanche of items shoved away willy-nilly.

- Keep like items together. One closet is for your cleaning supplies. The closet near your front door is for the family coats, sweaters, and hats. There is the toy closet. The closet filled with linens. The pantry closet. The closet filled with family heirlooms and mementos. The closet filled with clothing. And so on.

- If possible, make sure closets are brightly lit.

- Check the contents of each closet weekly. I can't tell you how common it is for people to open a closet after a few months—or years—and find that moths or mice have eaten away precious items, or mildew has set in. If your items are important enough to store, they are important enough to check on regularly.

- Don't overstuff closets. You should be able to see all—or at least most—of your items by standing at the open door of your closet.

- Get rid of anything you have not used in a year or that has no sentimental value.

- Keep the doors to closets clean and the hardware in good repair.

BASEMENTS, CELLARS, AND ATTICS

I have never lived in a home with a basement or an attic. But many of my cousins did, and I remember descending the dark, narrow cellar stairs to fetch a jar of jelly, preserves, or pickles for an aunt, or the creaky unstable steps up to a stale-smelling, dust-filled attic. If you have an underground or attic space, you can use it to enhance your home. Here's how:

- Give your space proper walls, a finished ceiling, and easy-to-clean floors. A finished room not only is more comfortable for a human to enjoy, but it is also safer. This is especially true if there is exposed insulation in your attic. As a bonus, finishing the room will also discourage animals from taking up residence.

- If a space is not tall enough for your tallest friend or family member to stand in, consider digging a foot or two deeper or raising the ceiling a bit.

- Watch air quality. Install ventilation, ceiling fans, or wall-mounted fans and access to outdoor air so there is always a supply of fresh oxygen.

- Get rid of the dampness. A dank space encourages mold and mildew growth and is unhealthy for human lungs.

- Use aromatherapy diffusers and vegetable-based essential oil candles to help improve the odor of underground spaces.

- Paint the space in a warm, light color.

- Install adequate lighting in your basement, cellar, or attic.

- If you'd like to use your basement or attic as storage space, install shelving, cabinets, and other places where items can be stored.

- Visit your cellar or attic once every week or two. If a raccoon takes up residence in your attic or a small hole appears in the ceiling, you can address this issue immediately before you have a problem that affects the rest of your home.

As you can see, creating a cozy home is not mysterious or difficult. It's good old-fashioned common sense, paired with some equally old-fashioned action. The payoff, however, is huge. Go through your rooms with the above tips and not only will your home look different, but it will also *feel* different—magic, warm, inviting. That, my friend, is hygge.

CHAPTER FIVE

COZY ENTERTAINING: TAPPING INTO TOGETHERNESS

There is nothing warmer than a welcome. It elicits feelings of acceptance, inclusion, safety, and comfort, which are at the heart of coziness. This feeling of warmth is so powerful that humans will do almost anything to be in its presence, from traveling across the country on a crowded plane, to fighting their way onto packed buses and subways, to spending hours driving in crosstown traffic. When we're basking in the warm welcome of friends and loved ones, everything else disappears—outdated furniture, a burnt side dish, dust bunnies hiding under sofas, a cramped dining room, a stained carpet, strangely colored throw pillows, or any other physical glitches we may have once viewed as flaws.

That feeling of welcome not only delights those who receive it, but it is also a salve to those who provide it. Research has shown that being kind to others can make you a happier person. I don't think it's a stretch to say that opening our homes to others is one of life's great kindnesses. In fact, enjoying your home with others is truly one of the most gratifying, cozy-creating actions available to you.

EASE INTO ENTERTAINING: CREATE A COZY FAMILY LIFE

If you're new to entertaining and are intimidated by the idea of opening your home to friends and acquaintances, creating weekly special time with your family—both nuclear and extended—is an easy place to start building your hospitality skills. Here are easy family-centric ideas for building your hospitality muscle.

Build together time into your weekly schedule. I grew up in a religion that required families to engage in something called Family Home Evening. Each and every Monday night, all families spent a couple of hours reading scripture together, doing a craft, talking, and snacking. Regardless of your religious beliefs, there are many benefits to scheduling weekly family time. Now my sons and I host Friday movie nights, where we come together (with home-popped popcorn and warmed lemonade) to watch movies. What home activity could you and your loved ones enjoy each week?

Develop common areas. These days, it's common for everyone to retreat to their rooms, where their computers are often located. Instead, try sitting with the people you live with—in the same room! You don't even have to talk! You can engage in reading, needlepoint, sewing on buttons, petting the dog, napping, or whatever you like.

Put away your devices. Hanging out in a room with other people does not work if you're staring at your phone. Worried about separation anxiety? I have a

charging station located on the kitchen counter where people can park their phones. People seem more willing to give up their phones when those devices are charging nearby.

Share both your time and your home. As we get busier, the number of people we allow into our homes usually shrinks, for all kinds of reasons, from a lack of cleanup time to simply having no energy to entertain. A life without guests, however, is not healthy—especially if you have children you've been entrusted to socialize. Choose one day a week when you or your children have friends over. Lessen your workload by lightly cleaning a few common areas, and then close off the rest of the house.

ENTERTAIN LIKE A DANE

Danes enjoy opening their homes to others for no reason other than to spend time together. There is no need for a special occasion or a holiday—inviting people over simply to hang out is all the reason necessary. Given this down-to-earth, practical view of entertaining, it probably won't surprise you that hygge entertaining is a comfy, cozy affair. Here are a few hygge pointers to get you started.

- Clean and tidy your home reasonably well, but don't make yourself crazy. Danes are neat, orderly people, but they are also easygoing. A few toys on the floor or dishes in the sink should not get in the way of having visitors over.

- Don't worry about entertainment. A lot of my American friends purchase games or toys for the little ones to play when they are together, or pull out board games or a movie for the adults. This is unthinkable to a Dane, who finds entertainment in the simple act of getting to know someone better. A more Danish way of looking at entertainment would be to put away the distractions and just talk and laugh together.

- Play music. It is not uncommon to hear some type of mood music playing softly in the background. To create a cozy atmosphere, Danes know to keep music lower than a human voice and to stick with instrumental-only melodies so there is nothing to compete with conversation.

- Light candles. Danes love candles of any kind. Before a guest arrives, it's not uncommon to find a Danish host quickly placing candles in various strategic spots (away from kids) around the home.

- Use throws and blankets. Danes like blankets and often will have a few draped on chairs or sofas. It's common to find guests curled on a sunny chair snuggled in a soft blanket.

- Don't go overboard with snacks. Food complements a visit, but it is never the reason people visit you. Danes like to think you visit them because you want to spend time with them, not because you want to be fed. A pot of coffee and a plate of three or five types of cookies are common Danish refreshments.

LOSE YOUR FEAR OF HOSTING

What if you like the *idea* of having visitors but are overcome with terror at the idea of actually having other people in your space? Maybe you don't have time to get your home company ready. Or you worry that once people stop by for a visit, you'll never be able to get rid of them. Reasons to avoid company abound: Feeding guests is too expensive or time-consuming. Your home is too small, run-down, or unfashionable. Your guests won't enjoy themselves. You don't know how to cook. One of these objections may strike a chord—or your reason may be something entirely different.

Whatever your concern, it is normal to feel a bit of panic around inviting people into your home. While there has not been a lot of research on "fear of hosting," there was an intriguing 2009 survey by the UK makers of After Eight® dinner mints. Researchers spoke with 1,007 people and found that 57 percent felt that entertaining friends for a meal was more nerve-racking than commuting to work, 24 percent claimed it was more uncomfortable than sitting through a job interview, and 44 percent said it was more anxiety-invoking than going to the bank to ask for a loan.

Opening your home to others does not have to be taxing, scary, or expensive. Here various hosting obstacles and ways to get around them.

Your home is too small to comfortably fit guests. Invite only the number of people you're comfortable with. Or, if you have a backyard, use it as an additional room. And don't worry if your walls need to be painted, your furniture is outdated, or there is something else about your home that makes you feel self-conscious. Simply invite those people you know won't judge you for the way your home looks right now.

You can't manage all the cleaning. What can you do to make things easier? I require my sons to help me clean, which is a great help. Further, I concentrate on tidying up the front of the home and simply block off the back of my apartment (where my office, the kids' room, and the master suite are located). This gives me less to clean. Feel free to throw quilts over stained areas of the sofa and use disposable plates, cups, and cutlery to make life easier. No one will care that they aren't eating on china or that they can't hang out in your bedroom.

You don't have the time or energy to entertain. Dinner parties and brunches require a lot of energy to host. Potluck dinners, dessert parties, friends-and-family movie nights with snacks, or simple invitations to come over Sunday afternoon for coffee, however, are a cinch. Buy whatever you can, ask people to bring food and drinks, and provide firm start and end times, so people know when they should be scooting off.

You cannot afford to host people. Think small, and see the paragraph above for ideas. Invite friends and their kids over for cookie decorating or a crafty play date, have a wine-tasting night and assign people specific varietals to bring, host a potluck dinner, or throw a picnic brunch in your backyard. Many of our ancestors did not have a lot of money, but they always had a lot of company. You don't need to go into debt to open your home to others.

You hate cooking or don't know how to cook. Cater your event, call the local pizza place, or buy everything. Or, focus your party around something other than food, such as a movie or a book discussion or a knitting night. Serve a variety of packaged and premade snack foods.

You don't know anyone interesting. Invite the most boring people you know. Ask them questions and listen closely for interesting answers.

You feel awkward around groups of people. Then start small with one, two, or three people. Entertaining can be as simple as inviting the nice lady next door over for afternoon tea.

EASY TREATS: DANISH BUTTER COOKIES

Danes are brilliant at creating unassuming items that seem simple but are positively addictive. These cookies are a delicious case in point. They can be made 2 days ahead, or you can store them to have on hand for future guests. Flatten the dough into four disks, place one or more in freezer wrap, and freeze for up to 3 months. Just defrost the dough before using.

MAKES 8 DOZEN COOKIES

4 cups all-purpose flour

1 teaspoon baking soda

1 pound salted butter, at room temperature

$3/4$ cup sugar

Pinch salt

Optional: Pinch cardamom powder

Optional: 3 to 4 tablespoons coarse sugar, such as turbinado, sanding sugar, or even colored sugar

1. Preheat the oven to 325°F.

2. Line 2 large baking sheets with parchment paper or foil.

3. Whisk together the flour and baking soda.

4. In the large bowl of a stand mixer outfitted with a paddle attachment, beat the butter until fluffy. Add the sugar, salt, and cardamom, if using.

5. Add the flour mixture, mixing until just combined. Divide the dough into four disks.

6. Roll each piece of dough between large sheets of waxed paper to about $1/8$ inch thick. Store each disk in the fridge for about 45 minutes or overnight to firm.

7. Using a 2-inch round cookie cutter, cut cookies. You can also use a pizza cutter or knife and cut 2-inch squares. Arrange 1 inch apart on prepared baking sheets.

8. Reroll the scraps and refrigerate for an additional 30 minutes. Cut more shapes.

9. If desired, sprinkle coarse sugar on the cookies.

10. Bake the cookies about 15 minutes, or until pale blond.

11. Cool on the sheets for 5 minutes, and then carefully slide onto racks to cool completely.

12. Allow the pans to cool completely before baking more cookies.

HOW TO CREATE AN INVITING LIFE

Your life is big—bigger than you know. You have room for work, play, and relaxation, both alone and with others. Get into the habit of seeing life as more than waking up, going to work, coming home, watching a screen, going to bed, and starting the cycle again the next day. Where are pockets of time that you can use to relax at home in the company of others? I look at my calendar each night, at the beginning of each week, and at the beginning of each month, searching for easy (emphasis on the word *easy*) opportunities to invite people to share my home life. Here are some of my favorites, none of which will make you broke or exhausted. I promise!

Make hospitality a habit. Invite one person to dinner or over for coffee or cocktails each month. Starting small helps build your hosting muscles and allows you to slowly build up comfort and confidence with having people in your space.

I encourage you to get your calendar out now and look at the next few months. Is there one day each month that you can earmark as entertaining day? Mark it on the calendar and plan to email an invitation two or three weeks in advance (see page 90 for an invitation template).

Start a book club, a wine-tasting group, or something else that meets regularly. Forming a club or group gives you an easy excuse to have people in your home. Because you will be focused on club topics, there is no pressure to serve over-the-top food or have a spotless home. Guests are there for the meeting, not to assess your hosting skills.

Go informal. I adore the idea of formal dinner parties, with printed and mailed invitations, five-course meals, an ambitious guest list, and a strategically created seating plan. But for most of us, the idea of a formal dinner party is not only undoable, it is downright overwhelming. You can still be the hostess with the mostest without ever snail-mailing an invitation or creating a seating chart. Call, text, or send an invite over social media to desired guests. Include the event's date, start and end times, directions if appropriate, and anything else you think a person needs to know.

Involve your partner, kids, or anyone else you live with. All three of my kids are foodies who love planning, making, and eating elaborate meals. Each month we think of someone who has done something wonderful for one of us and invite that person to a dinner of my kids' making. In my invitation, I clearly state that this is a project the boys are in charge of: "My sons would love you to join us for a dinner that they are planning, cooking, and serving." This not only allows my children to practice their meal-planning and cooking skills but also gives them the ongoing opportunity to socialize with someone they may not normally take the time to get to know.

Host a regular potluck. People love to show off their cooking. Allowing people to bring dishes ensures there will be a range of chic and eclectic serving containers, a diversity of cooking skills, and a variety of people (and dishes) sharing a common space. It is a great way for those who aren't jazzed by formal dinners—or who are uncomfortable with their kitchen skills—to open their homes to others.

"Small cheer and great welcome makes a merry feast!"
—William Shakespeare

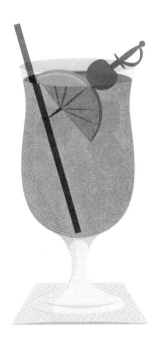

THE INVITATION TEMPLATE

Feel awkward about inviting an acquaintance to your home? Wondering how to get started? Customize this quick-and-easy invitation template.

Dear Friend,

I hope you are well!

It's been a while since we've spent time together. I would love to have you over to tea on the 17th. Are you available between 2 and 4 p.m. on that Sunday?

I am at 123 Main Street, apartment 2. If you're driving, there is parking on the street. The Metro Bus stops a half block away on the corner of Main Street and Broadway, if that is easier.

Do let me know if you have a favorite tea or if you have any dietary restrictions. Just a heads-up in case you have allergies: we do have a dog and cat, but they'll be shut away in the back of the apartment.

I am looking forward to hanging out with you!

Best,
Stephanie
212-555-1234

THE DARK SIDE OF COCOONING

I first came across the word *cocooning* in an undergrad sociology class in the early 1990s. The class had been assigned Faith Popcorn's book *The Popcorn Report*, about how trends and lifestyle movements were changing the way Americans lived. Cocooning was defined by Popcorn as "the impulse to stay inside when the outside gets too tough and scary." Doesn't it make sense that people would want this calm, safe warmth more than the impersonal, cold, frenzied stressors of the outside world?

Decades have passed since Faith Popcorn coined the term, but for some of us, cocooning is just as attractive today as it ever was—an effective way to feel safe and grounded in our harried world. But like many things, it comes with a dark side, one that we're beginning to see more of in the 21st century: isolation.

Unfortunately, loneliness is common in the United States. According to a 2016 Harris Poll of more than 2,000 people surveyed in the US, 72 percent reported feeling lonely at times—and almost one-third experienced loneliness at least once *every* week. Not only does isolation feel bad, but it also has negative effects on both individuals and society. Consider the following research reports, taken from dozens of studies on loneliness.

- In a report published in 2017, researchers from King's College London used data from the Environmental Risk Longitudinal Twin Study, a study of 2,232 twins born in England and Wales in 1994 and 1995, who were evaluated at ages 7, 10, 12, and 18. Those who reported feeling lonely were more likely to experience poor sleep quality, daytime tiredness, and poor concentration than their non-lonely counterparts.

○ A 2017 study led by researchers from the University of Houston and Rice University in Texas asked 160 participants to complete a loneliness survey. After exposing the participants to a cold virus, those who ranked themselves most lonely were most likely to succumb to it.

○ Loneliness is a significant predictor of poor health. In a 2010 survey of 3,012 people ages 45 and older, commissioned by AARP, those who rated their health as "excellent" were around half as likely to be lonely than those who rated their health as "poor" (25 versus 55 percent).

○ In a 2016 study, researchers from Brigham and Women's Hospital and Harvard Medical School identified a marker of early Alzheimer's disease in the brains of seniors with greater self-reported loneliness. Researchers surveyed 79 adults—none of whom had symptoms of Alzheimer's disease—about their levels of loneliness and isolation. Using brain imaging, the researchers then measured amyloid protein levels in each of the participants' brains. Amyloid proteins can form clumps called plaques, which are considered a hallmark of Alzheimer's. Compared with participants with low cortical amyloid levels, subjects with high amyloid levels were seven and a half times more likely to report feeling lonely, the researchers found.

If you don't take steps to develop a social network, you will not have a social network. It is that simple. Stretch out of your comfort zone to interact with the people around you. Not only will a strong social network strengthen your mental and physical health—and that of your loved ones—you'll also find life to be brighter, easier, and more enjoyable when spent in community with others.

CHAPTER SIX

COZY CUISINE: COMFORT AT THE TABLE

For many of us, home-crafted meals are an afterthought. We snack too much, munching on the go instead of sitting down and eating "in a proper way," as my grandmother would say. As a result, we often eat too much sugar or sodium or too many carbs and forget just how much we've already put in our bodies. After all, it's hard to keep track of your food intake (and even your level of hunger) when your focus is not on the food but on getting yourself somewhere fast because you're late.

I am convinced that this whole concept of eating on the go is an American thing. We're the country of fast food, drive-up windows, and snack-sized packages. But I ask you to really think about this: when it comes to food, taking the time to make and eat meals is an act of deep self-care. It is a celebration. It is a simple, significant approach to create warmth, memories, and magic. Your life will change in powerful ways when you commit to assembling some or all of your own meals.

THE HYGGE GUIDE TO CHOOSING TABLEWARE

Meals aren't just about the food. What you use to serve and eat your food matters, too. The Danes are known for their tableware, and if there is one thing I learned when I was growing up as a Danish American, it is how to put together a functional, streamlined, attractive kitchen, using beautiful pieces that show off your sense of style.

If you are building a kitchen that supports a life of comfort and ease, you'll want enough flatware, cups, plates, bowls, and glasses to serve meals on and to have ready for entertaining—but not so many pieces that your home becomes cluttered. Here are some hygge-inspired recommendations for building a kitchen that allows you to pleasurably create handcrafted food.

Watch the size. One of the easiest ways to encourage healthy portions is to use average-sized (or even small) plates, bowls, and glasses. Further, those 12-plus-inch plates are impossible to squeeze into most dishwashers and often don't fit into standard-sized kitchen cabinets. Stick to dinner plates that are a maximum of 8$\frac{1}{2}$ to 10$\frac{1}{2}$ inches.

Don't overbuy. To avoid kitchen clutter, watch out for "twosies syndrome"—thinking you need two different versions of the same item, such as two types of tumblers, two styles of bowls, and so forth. In Denmark, something must be functional in order to be considered beautiful. Find pieces that function in many food-oriented situations—choose one type of dinner plate, skip the salad plates, limit yourself to one type of bowl (a low bowl can double as a salad plate), one type of drinking glass, one size of wine glass, and one type of cup or mug.

Choose your color and pattern wisely. Look at your tableware color palettes and designs. Does everything work together? If it doesn't, you'll be tempted to purchase and store another set of tableware just for entertaining or for holidays. Make things easy on yourself and make sure all of your tableware is complementary, so it can be used for every occasion. You can never go wrong with all-white dishes, although any one or two solid colors can work. For example, my dinner plates and teacups are lime green, and my soup bowls and saucers are tangerine orange.

All your dishes, glasses, and utensils should be dishwasher-safe. Yes, bone china edged in 24-karat gold is stunning. But it is not practical. On this Danes and Americans agree. Items that don't make extra work for you and your guests are more functional than high-maintenance items that require fiddly care.

Open stock may be your best option. Many companies sell place settings. While convenient, if you're trying to reduce clutter, these premade options may add to the chaos. Instead, go open stock (buy individual pieces instead of purchasing an entire preassembled place setting) and choose only what you need.

Use the same tableware for everyday dining and special occasions. Stick to the same tableware for all occasions, from weekend wine and cheese with your book club to family breakfasts to formal holiday dinners. Opt for something you love that can be dressed up or down using napkins, tablecloths, and centerpieces. You'll save space on storage and keep a cleaner, neater home.

Buy what you need. Purchasing settings for 8, 10, or 12 is the norm, but your needs may be different. Are you a couple who hosts monthly 10-person dinner parties? A family of 4 whose home is holiday central for the relatives? A dedicated singleton who hates the idea of having more than three people in your apartment at any given time? Consider what you need to support your daily eating and entertaining habits.

But do not buy more than you need. Anything you buy, you must store. And by store, I don't mean in a special closet in a back bedroom somewhere. If you don't have enough kitchen cupboard space to house your dishes, limit yourself to only as many place settings as you have room for. You can always rent tableware if you are throwing a large dinner party or holiday meal.

Keep all your tableware in your kitchen or (if you must) your pantry or dining room. If you have more dishes, silverware, or glassware than space—or if you are tempted to keep items in that back bedroom mentioned above—your tableware has stopped being useful and is now clutter.

KEEPING AND DISPLAYING FOOD

For many people, food enjoys one of the most visible positions in the home. This can be wonderful when the food is decorative and healthy—and less so when it comes in ugly cartons and garishly colored packages that lead to an unpleasant, cluttered look. Use food as a decorative force for good with these tips.

- Invest in beautiful, classically shaped food storage canisters. Transfer staples such as flour, grains, beans, and sweeteners to attractive containers.

- Do the same with ingredients that must be kept in the fridge or freezer, by using beautiful cold-temperature storage containers for all of your must-be-refrigerated items.

- Don't keep packaged food on the counter, on top of the fridge, on the dining room table, or on any other visible space. A vase of lemons and limes looks inviting wherever you place it; a box of cereal will only give your home a cluttered look. Place all packaged food behind cupboard or pantry doors.

- Choose cupboards with solid doors over glass cupboards or open kitchen shelving, especially if you keep commercially packaged food in your kitchen.

- Keep your fridge, freezer, stove, and cupboards as clean as you can. A "pretty clean" kitchen is much more inviting than a dirty one.

- Colorful magnets, kids' artwork, coupons, bills, calendars, and so forth do not belong stuck to the fridge. Your kitchen will look cleaner, warmer, and more inviting if you find another place for these items.

MINIMALIST COOKING FOR MAXIMUM ENJOYMENT

Most Americans don't have a lot of time to spend in the kitchen. This has contributed to a $200 billion fast food industry in the US (as of 2015), up from $6 billion in 1970, according to the *Fast Food Industry Analysis 2017*, an industry report by the organization FranchiseHelp.

I'm not saying that spending money on takeout and other convenience foods is a bad thing. But if you learn how to make a few basic items and set aside weekly time for food prep, your life will change. Healthy, appetizing breakfasts, lunches, dinners, and snacks will be easy and fast to put together. Your family will experience the old-fashioned pleasures of eating real food without you being chained to some of the old-fashioned torments of creating food. For ideas on how this could work for you, I offer a glimpse into my own cooking system, inspired by generations of traditional Danish and American cuisine. I call it "minimalist cooking for maximum enjoyment." You'll find that these comforting dishes not only free up your time and scent your home with comforting aromas, they also provide an important warmth—all of which work together to create maximum coziness with a surprisingly small amount of effort.

EASY ROAST CHICKEN

Roasting a chicken is one of those things that I required my sons to know by the time they were 16—along with how to make fried and scrambled eggs, toast, tea, a medium-rare steak, burgers, and panfried fish. It is a foundational recipe that can feed you in many ways. This recipe can be jazzed up with spices, herbs, or additional (or different) veggies.

MAKES 6 TO 8 SERVINGS

1 (4^1/$_2$- to 6-pound) roasting chicken

Salt and pepper

1 bunch fresh thyme or a few sprigs each of any of these: parsley, chives, marjoram, thyme, rosemary, oregano, and sage

1 lemon, cut in half

1 head garlic, cut in half crosswise

3 tablespoons melted butter, coconut oil, extra virgin olive oil, bacon fat, or another oil, divided

1 large yellow onion, thickly sliced, or 2 cleaned and trimmed leeks, roughly chopped

4 carrots or parsnips (or a mix), cut into 2-inch chunks

1. Preheat the oven to 425°F.
2. If the chicken came with giblets and the neck, remove and discard them. Also remove any excess fat.
3. Pat the chicken dry, inside and out.
4. Rub salt and pepper over the chicken's inside cavity.
5. Place the thyme, lemon, and garlic inside the cavity of the chicken.
6. Rub the outside of the chicken with 2 tablespoons of the melted butter, and then sprinkle with a generous amount of salt and pepper.
7. If you'd like, tuck the wing tips under the chicken's body and tie the chicken legs together with kitchen string.
8. Place the onion and carrots in a roasting pan and toss with the remaining 1 tablespoon of melted butter and salt and pepper.
9. Rest the chicken on top of the prepared vegetables in the roasting pan.
10. Roast the chicken for 1^1/$_2$ hours, or until the juices run clear when you insert a sharp paring knife between a leg and thigh.
11. Remove from the oven, cover with foil, and allow it to cool for about 15 minutes before slicing. Or, allow it to completely cool, wrap in foil, and store in the fridge for up to 4 days.

FISH BAKED IN COCONUT MILK

This recipe is so versatile that I have included versions of it in several of my cookbooks. Use salmon, tuna, or your favorite mild white fish. It all works. Feel free to play with the veggies, spices, and herbs.

MAKES 4 SERVINGS

4 teaspoons lemon juice

6 tablespoons liquid coconut oil, divided

Salt

2 pounds thick fish fillets or steaks (halibut, cod, or salmon)

2 cups finely chopped onion

2 teaspoons minced garlic

2 teaspoons minced fresh ginger

1 teaspoon minced green serrano or jalapeño chile pepper

1 cup chopped tomatoes (fresh or drained canned)

5 teaspoons ground coriander

1 teaspoon ground cumin

$1/4$ teaspoon cayenne pepper

$1/4$ teaspoon ground black pepper

$1/4$ teaspoon ground turmeric

1 teaspoon dried parsley

$1/2$ cup canned coconut milk

Optional: $1/4$ cup chopped fresh parsley, chives, or cilantro, for garnish

1. Preheat the oven to 350°F.

2. Lightly grease a baking dish large enough to hold the fish in a single layer. Set aside.

3. Whisk together the lemon juice, 2 tablespoons of the coconut oil, and a pinch of salt in a small bowl. Set aside.

4. Cut the fillets crosswise into 2-inch-wide strips. Rub the fish with the lemon juice mixture, place in the prepared baking dish, cover, and refrigerate for 1 hour.

5. In medium frying pan, over medium-high heat, fry the onion in the remaining 4 tablespoons of coconut oil until the edges are browned.

6. Add the garlic, ginger, and chile pepper, and stir over medium heat for 2 minutes.

7. Add the tomatoes, coriander, cumin, cayenne pepper, black pepper, turmeric, parsley, and $1^{1}/_{4}$ teaspoons salt, and fry, stirring until the tomato breaks down into a chunky sauce.

8. Add the coconut milk and simmer about 5 minutes, until the mixture becomes thick.

9. Remove the fish from the refrigerator, uncover, and bake for 10 minutes.

10. Remove the fish from oven, pour the sauce over the fish, cover tightly with foil, and return to the oven for 15 to 20 minutes or until the fish is opaque.

11. Garnish, if desired, with chopped herbs.

SLOW COOKER BEANS

I use my slow cooker about three times each week, for beans, shredded chicken, pulled pork, beef, bone broth, and more. This recipe for beans brilliantly allows you to make a batch of this important (and versatile) food for use in all kinds of dishes, from salads to grain pilafs to soups to burritos and more. Use any kind of bean you'd like and feel free to play around with the herbs and spices.

MAKES ABOUT 4 CUPS

½ pound dry beans, such as black beans, pintos, chickpeas, etc., picked through to remove debris or discolored beans

Enough water or broth (or a combination of the two) to cover the beans during cooking

2 to 4 garlic cloves, minced

½ teaspoon salt, if using water

Optional: 1 to 3 teaspoons of your favorite spice

Optional: ½ to 2 tablespoons of your favorite dried herb

1. Place the beans in a large bowl and cover with cold water. Place in the refrigerator overnight to soak. This step helps remove much of the beans' oligosaccharides, a complex sugar that is difficult for humans to digest.

2. When you're ready to cook the beans, remove them from the fridge, transfer them to a colander, and run cool water over them for a few minutes to rinse away any vestiges of oligosaccharides.

3. Set a slow cooker to its lowest setting and add the soaked and rinsed beans.

4. Pour enough water or broth over the beans to cover by 2 inches. Add the minced garlic, which will not only flavor the beans, but also help improve their digestibility.

5. Add salt, if using, and any spices or herbs.

6. Cook the beans on low for 5 hours.

7. Check the beans for doneness. Cook longer, if needed, adding water if the beans are beginning to dry out. Check every 30 minutes, as needed.

8. Once the beans are done, remove them from the slow cooker and drain any excess liquid. I like to measure the beans into 1-cup serving containers and store in the fridge for up to 5 days to be used in recipes throughout the week. I also freeze some of the beans for future use.

SLOW COOKER BEEF

This delicious recipe uses the slow cooker, making it an excellent timesaver. My family eats this as is with roast vegetables and mashed potatoes, stashes it in tortillas and calls it a taco, scatters it on nachos, tucks it into sandwich rolls, and more. I find this recipe particularly easy because it doesn't require you to sear the meat over the stove before adding it to a slow cooker.

MAKES 8 SERVINGS

1 (3- to 4-pound) boneless beef roast (chuck or round roast)

1 cup beef broth

$1/2$ cup balsamic vinegar

1 tablespoon Worcestershire sauce

1 tablespoon shoyu or tamari

1 tablespoon brown sugar, honey, or maple syrup

4 garlic cloves, minced

1. Place the beef into the insert of a slow cooker.
2. In small mixing bowl, whisk together the broth, vinegar, Worcestershire sauce, shoyu, and brown sugar. Pour over the beef and set the timer for 6 hours on low.
3. Check the beef at 6 hours. If it is still pink, allow it to cook for an additional 30 minutes and then recheck.
4. Remove the beef with tongs and transfer it to a serving plate.
5. Collect the liquid that has accumulated in the slow cooker and whisk to make it smooth. Pour over the beef.
6. Slice the beef into servings and transfer to 1- or 2-cup refrigerator-safe containers.

ROASTED VEGETABLES

I make this differently each weekend, using whatever I've brought home from the market. In other words, the ingredients are not set in stone. Don't have 1 pound of potatoes? Use ½ pound of yellow carrots and ½ pound of trimmed kohlrabi. Did you just buy some great-looking red peppers and a few fennel bulbs? Use them instead of a vegetable you don't have (or don't like or have an intolerance to). You can also play with the oils—pecan or walnut oil works well—and the herbs. You can even add a shake of your favorite spice with the salt and pepper. Cumin is great, as is ground chipotle, star anise, dry mustard—you get the idea!

MAKES 8 SERVINGS

1 pound potatoes, unpeeled, scrubbed, cut into 1-inch pieces

1 pound celery root (celeriac), peeled and cut into 1-inch pieces

1 pound rutabagas, peeled and cut into 1-inch pieces

1 pound carrots, peeled and cut into 1-inch pieces

1 pound parsnips, peeled and cut into 1-inch pieces

2 onions, cut into 1-inch pieces

2 leeks (white and pale green parts only), cut into 1-inch pieces

2 tablespoons chopped fresh rosemary (or 1 tablespoon fresh rosemary and 1 tablespoon another fresh herb)

½ cup extra virgin olive oil

Salt and pepper

10 garlic cloves, peeled

1. Position one rack in the bottom third of the oven and one rack in the center of the oven. Preheat the oven to 400°F.

2. Combine all ingredients except the garlic in very large bowl; toss to coat. Season generously with salt and pepper.

3. Divide the vegetable mixture between 2 shallow baking pans.

4. Place one pan on each oven rack. Roast 30 minutes, stirring occasionally. Reverse the positions of the baking pans. Add 5 garlic cloves to each baking pan.

5. Continue to roast until all vegetables are tender and brown in spots, stirring and turning the vegetables occasionally, about 45 minutes longer. (The vegetables can be prepared 4 hours ahead of serving. Let stand on the baking pans at room temperature. Rewarm in a 450°F oven until heated through, about 15 minutes.)

6. Transfer the roasted vegetables to a large bowl and serve.

ROASTED PORK TENDERLOINS

Slices of lean, succulent pork make a great dinner paired with a grain, a cooked vegetable, and a fresh garden salad. But I like to save my pork tenderloin for sandwiches, stir-fries, burrito bowls, and other weekday meals.

4 tablespoons balsamic vinegar

4 tablespoons extra virgin olive oil

8 garlic cloves, minced

Salt and pepper, to taste

2 teaspoons cumin

1 teaspoon red pepper flakes

$^1/_2$ teaspoon dried rosemary

$^1/_2$ teaspoon dried thyme

$4^1/_2$ pounds pork tenderloin (about 3 or 4 average-sized pork tenderloins)

1. Preheat the oven to 425°F.

2. In a small bowl, whisk together the vinegar, oil, garlic, salt and pepper, cumin, red pepper flakes, rosemary, and thyme.

3. Place the tenderloins on a rimmed baking sheet and rub with the vinegar-spice mixture.

4. Roast in the oven for 20 to 30 minutes, or until done. If you have a meat thermometer, insert it into a thick spot of the pork and see if it reads 145°F. Or spear with a paring knife and check to see if pinkness has gone. If not, allow to cook for 5 more minutes before rechecking.

5. Remove from the oven and allow to sit for 5 to 10 minutes before carving.

A BARE-BONES COOKING EQUIPMENT GUIDE

A cluttered kitchen looks unappetizing, is hard to keep sanitary, and is difficult (or, in some cases, dangerous) to work in. In general, these items are all you need to easily turn out wonderful meals:

- The biggies: An oven with a stovetop, a refrigerator with a freezer, and—if you have room and can afford it—a dishwasher.

- Knives and accessories: A well-made chef's knife that feels great in your hand, a paring knife, and a serrated knife for cutting bread and tomatoes.

- Countertop appliances: Limit yourself to no more than three, such as a juicer, a blender, and a coffeepot. Keep less-used appliances off the counter in a dedicated kitchen cabinet, and pull them out only when you use them.

- Pots, pans, and other stoveware: Most of us use the same pan and the same two pots over and over, which is why most people really only need a frying/sauté pan, a small or medium pot, and a pot that is large enough to cook pasta and make stock. Keep these heavily used pots and pans on your stovetop; tuck away others in a cupboard.

- Bakeware: As with pots, most of us use the same few baking pans. If you're in the market for a few new pieces, I recommend a 24-cup muffin tin, two 9-inch cake pans, two baking sheets (used for everything from free-form bread loaves to cookies to fish patties), a 9 × 11-inch glass pan, and a 2-quart casserole dish.

- Kitchen helpers: Let the foods you eat regularly guide your choices. Keep items you use daily within easy reach. For instance, in a large vase near the knife block, I keep a vegetable peeler, a citrus reamer, a ladle, a large flat spoon, a wooden spoon, and a Danish whisk. Your less-used kitchen helpers can remain out of sight in a drawer or cupboard.

SOUP IS GOOD FOOD

For many Danes—and Americans, too—soup is the epitome of hygge. It's cozy, warming, comforting, and nourishing. And, fortunately for the cook, it's easy and pleasurable to make—even for people who don't know how or don't like to cook. That's why most Danes make soup almost daily. In fact, it's rare for a Danish kitchen to be without something simmering on a back burner, ready to be enjoyed when the children get home from school and everyone returns from work.

Danes are not recipe followers, preferring to throw dishes together using whatever they have on hand. This soup blueprint—with three variations—honors Scandinavians' love of creative cooking, while providing just enough direction to ensure that you'll always end up with something so delicious that your loved ones won't stop raving about your soup-making skills.

CARROT-GINGER-ALMOND BISQUE

I made a lot of winter veggie–nut butter soups when my oldest son was an infant. This carrot and almond-butter version was his favorite. I love it, too. It's incredibly economical and outrageously easy.

MAKES 5 SERVINGS

2 tablespoons butter, coconut oil, almond oil, avocado oil, or extra virgin olive oil

3 cups chopped carrots

$1/2$ cup chopped onion

$1/2$ cup chopped celery

2 teaspoons minced fresh ginger

1 or 2 garlic cloves, minced

4 cups chicken or vegetable broth

$1/2$ teaspoon or more pumpkin pie spice (or any combination of cinnamon and as much or as little allspice, ground ginger, and/or cloves as sounds delicious to you; you can even add a teeny bit of freshly ground mace or nutmeg—but not too much, or you'll get a bitter taste)

$1/2$ teaspoon salt, or to taste, depending upon how salty your broth is

$1/4$ cup almond butter (any type is fine)

$1 1/2$ tablespoons natural soy sauce (shoyu or tamari), or increase the salt to 1 teaspoon

Black pepper, to taste

Optional: A squeeze or more of lemon juice

Optional: Chopped almonds, for garnish

Optional: Chopped fresh parsley, for garnish

Optional: Cinnamon, for garnish

1. Warm the butter in a large soup pot over medium heat. Add the carrots, onion, celery, fresh ginger, and garlic. Sauté until the vegetables are just softened and the onions begin to get translucent.

2. Add the broth and simmer, about 20 minutes, until the carrots are tender.

3. Cool to room temperature.

4. In a blender (do this in batches if necessary), puree the soup with the pumpkin pie spice, salt, almond butter, soy sauce, black pepper, and lemon juice, if using. Continue blending until the soup is silky smooth.

5. Garnish the finished soup with chopped almonds and/or chopped parsley and a dusting of cinnamon, if desired.

Note: If you like your carrot soup a bit on the sweet side, blend in a few teaspoons of natural sugar or maple syrup.

WINTER SQUASH AND HAZELNUT BISQUE

Follow the Carrot-Ginger-Almond Bisque recipe (page 109), with these ingredient changes:

....

Reduce the carrots to 1/2 cup.

Add 3 cups of cubed winter quash (such as butternut, hubbard, or kobacha).

Add a pinch of freshly ground nutmeg (or use allspice).

Increase the fresh ginger to 1 tablespoon.

Use pure hazelnut/filbert butter instead of the almond butter.

Reduce the soy sauce to 1 tablespoon.

Add 1/2 tablespoon Grade B maple syrup.

....

SWEET POTATO AND PEANUT BISQUE

Follow the Carrot-Ginger-Almond Bisque recipe (page 109), with these ingredient changes:

....

Reduce the carrots to 1/2 cup.

Add 3 cups of peeled and cubed deeply colored sweet potatoes.

Add a pinch of freshly ground allspice.

Increase the fresh ginger to 1 tablespoon.

Use natural peanut butter instead of the almond butter.

Reduce the soy sauce to 1 tablespoon.

Add 1/2 tablespoon of Grade B maple syrup.

MINDFUL EATING RULES

So often we eat mindlessly, while working on the computer, watching TV, or on the run. But the pleasure of eating lies in slowing down and fully experiencing all of the elements of food. Here are some tips for more mindful snacks and meals.

Do not eat standing up. Ever. You are not livestock. Humans, to fully digest their food and create the chemical that tells the brain it's full, like to be seated. If you want something and cannot sit down, then do not eat it until you can.

Do not snack in front of a phone, computer, or television screen. Eating while answering emails, talking on the phone, or anything else is a form of multitasking. Concentrate instead on fueling your body. Your body will reward this attention by telling you the moment it has consumed enough. Your senses will receive a well-deserved dive into the sight, aroma, taste, and texture of your food. And you'll have given yourself a meditative moment to enjoy the relaxing pleasure of eating.

Chew thoroughly. Did you know that most humans chew their food an average of eight times? This is unfortunate, because the more you chew, the more thoroughly you break down your food. Not only does this help in utilizing food's nutrients, but it also encourages you to slow down and enjoy what you have.

Choose a snack that has both fiber and protein. Snacks such as carrots and hummus, veggie strips and white bean dip, or celery with almond butter will fill you up and give you energizing protein, which in turn will lessen your desire for mindless between-meal grazing.

(continued on next page)

Consider where you eat. To avoid mindless snacking and really focus on your food, avoid eating in environments that foster distraction, such as your car or loud spaces. Also avoid eating in messy places, as your food takes on the energy of the space you eat in.

Do not eat straight from a bag, box, or carton. Take out a portion and serve yourself regally. As my grandmother used to say, "How you eat matters. Would the queen of England eat the way you're eating?" It's a question I often ask myself when I am tempted to filch leftovers from my kid's finished plates while doing the dishes or grab a handful of food while vacuuming.

CREATING TOGETHERNESS WHEN YOU CAN'T HAVE A FAMILY MEAL

In theory, the family meal is a beautiful thing. Joining together at the end of the day allows family members to reconnect over an activity that humans have been enjoying since the beginning of time: eating together. The family meal also makes practical sense, allowing parents to spend time with their moody teenager, ensure their elementary school–aged kid is eating enough veggies, and teach little ones valuable table manners. Further, the family meal makes for less cleanup: serve food once and clean. The kitchen can then close until the next day.

Real life, however, is often wildly different from the fantasy you read about on parenting blogs or see on *Leave It to Beaver* reruns.

These days, many people work well into the dinner hour. Children, as well, are busy later into the day than their 20th-century counterparts, with sports, rehearsals, test prep, and other extracurricular activities.

To keep things cozy while accommodating different schedules, in our household, we have hit upon a compromise: two dinner periods, one meal choice. The first time slot is at 6:15. I sit down with a glass of water and keep whoever is eating company. I get a chance to hear how my sons' days have gone and watch how they are eating. Afterward, the boys help with their dishes; the serving platters stay on the table for the next shift, which is at 7:30. Anyone not eating is asked to respect the diners' desire for quiet by staying out of the dining room. After the 7:30 meal is over, all uneaten food is packed into the next day's lunches or stored, and all dishes are done.

While you may hit upon your own solution, here are some ideas you may find helpful for creating togetherness when you can't all be at the table.

- Do not make different meals for different diners. Regardless of when people eat, they get the same meal as those who ate earlier. Try to make one item—an entrée or side dish—that each family member enjoys.

- Make foods that can withstand hanging around for a while. Save fiddly foods (such as soufflés) or foods that must be eaten warm (such as fish) for holidays or other special occasions when everyone eats together.

- Sit down with any stragglers while they eat, or putter in the kitchen while your straggler eats.

- If dinner is a hard meal to eat together during the week, instate a regular Saturday pizza night or Sunday midday meal, or have a family breakfast. The time of your family meal doesn't matter.

- Ditch the family meal for a post-dinner family snack. Our family enjoys a long-standing Friday movie night with homemade popcorn and hot lemonade for anyone who happens to be home. Even my teenagers try not to miss this tradition.

GROCERY SHOPPING THE DANISH WAY

One of my favorite things to do when I travel is to watch locals shop for food. Every culture has its grocery shopping quirks. I've noticed that in some countries—the US, Canada, and Australia—people visit mammoth, soup-to-nuts supermarkets once a week for large amounts of food. People in other countries—such as France, Italy, and Japan—stop by specialty stores several times a week to pick up a small amount of perishable foods, such as veggies, fish, and meat. Is one way better than another? Not at all. But if you'd like to transform your shopping from a drudgery-filled chore to a lighthearted, sensory-pleasing part of your week, let me share with you how Danes shop.

Shop first, plan meals second. Any coupon website or frugal parenting blog will tell you to make a meal plan, and then shop accordingly. I disagree. Throughout Europe, South America, and Asia, shoppers look to see what items are fresh and priced well, buy those things, and then cook according to what they purchased. While this contradicts the way many Americans have been told to shop, it will save you money and ensure that you and your family enjoy the largest possible variety of fresh food.

Shop once or twice a week. Many Americans adhere to once-a-month or once-a-fortnight shopping, stocking up on additive-filled foods and frozen ingredients. Danes don't believe in stuffing a home with food that's meant to be eaten over the course of a few weeks. It is healthier for your body and your spirit to invest in fresh whole foods meant to be enjoyed immediately.

Find a good butcher. If you eat meat (poultry included), a good butcher can be a real money saver. A butcher can also expose you and your family to types and cuts of fresh meats that you may not otherwise try.

Find a good fishmonger. As with a good butcher, a good fishmonger is invaluable.

Frequent your farmers market. Eating local food in season is a powerful way to celebrate life. Danes use the appearance of certain foods to commemorate Earth's seasons: nettles and rhubarb in the spring, berries in the summer, apples and squash in the fall, roots in the winter. Enjoying seasonal food with your family connects you to the earth and creates a sense of awareness around and gratitude for what it creates for us.

Always buy a bouquet of flowers. Danish kitchen tables always feature a vase of blooms. Why? Flowers lighten the mood and add warmth to the home. If you are on a budget, try an inexpensive bunch of baby's breath or mini carnations. If money is especially tight, give your children colored paper and bamboo sticks or pipe cleaners and have them create a "bouquet" for the table.

Don't buy in bulk. Having a lot of food sitting about creates clutter and, for some people, can lead to overeating. Additionally, large amounts of stored food can lead to food waste. Have you ever bought five of something and only used one or two by the time the items expired? I have, too.

Shop the perimeter, where most of the produce, meat, fish, bulk grains, and dairy are. Avoid the interior aisles filled with convenience foods. You know the ones—they contain unhealthy, sugary cereals and any number of cookies, chips, canned soups, boxed pasta meals, and so forth.

Shop early or late. A cozy life leaves time for the things you care about. There's no need to spend your valuable time trudging behind people in a market or waiting on a checkout line. Visiting the market at off hours, at the beginning or end of your day, can save time—minutes or hours you can use to read, hang out with your kids, or squeeze in another load of laundry.

Food is an enormous part of how humans create and offer comfort to others. Use this beautiful practice as a powerful—and easy—way to create coziness in your life while fostering connections with those around you. You will be delighted at the results.

CHAPTER SEVEN

COZY CELEBRATIONS: HOLIDAYS AND SPECIAL OCCASIONS

Have you ever stopped to think about why you love special occasions? Why do weddings, birthday parties, anniversaries, first days of school, and baby showers leave you feeling happy?

I think fun is the reason. Celebrations are fun, and fun is something that motivates humans. Think about how you look forward to reliving the warmth and joy you remember from celebrations past. Some of these traditions are religious or cultural traditions: at New Year's we toast with Champagne; at Thanksgiving we eat turkey, stuffing, and cranberry sauce. Other rituals may be special family traditions, such as receiving a silver dollar in exchange for a lost baby tooth or visiting the cemetery on Memorial Day to remember the veterans in your town who have passed on.

In today's uncomfortably frenzied and ever-changing world, these commemorations are more important than ever before. Festive traditions ground us and help us organize our lives amid constant change. Enjoying long-held holiday traditions provides a feeling of safety as well as important continuity with our past, reminding us that life is bigger than we are. Celebratory traditions also bind us to one another in the most pleasant way possible.

I moved around a lot in my childhood—between countries, states, cities, and neighborhoods. For me, some of my warmest, happiest moments were each December when we would return to my grandparents' home. No matter what my American friends' families were doing, my Danish family continued on with the same very Danish Christmas rituals they had performed for generations. On the afternoon of Christmas Eve, my grandfather, father, and a few cousins would set out to find a Christmas tree on the land around my grandparents' home. While the grown-ups would choose and fell the tree, my cousins and I would gather wild holly, mistletoe, and pinecones to decorate the home. Then we would decorate the tree with traditional handmade Danish ornaments, such as paper hearts. This was one of the few times of year that I knew the rules. The feeling of comfort and self-assuredness this gave me was unlike anything I knew in my everyday life.

This sense of safety and warmth is the same for every person who has ever indulged in a family tradition. It is a mainstay of hygge and of coziness. Each person on this planet deserves such joy.

TRADITIONS THAT WORK FOR YOU: CELEBRATIONS MADE CALM

The best kind of tradition is one that you enjoy. Few of us enjoy things that are overly complicated, expensive, fiddly, or that take a lot of time to pull off. This is why so many of the traditions that our parents—and their parents—grew up with are so challenging. We simply have a differ-ent relationship to time today. Ignoring that is setting ourselves up for frustration.

Back in the day, a person wasn't expected to fit so much into 24 hours. Even if there were no time-saving conveniences to make sewing holiday outfits or whipping up festive desserts easy, humans had the time to devote to these tasks. Today, we're expected to get a lot done each day—taking time out to fashion homemade Valentine's Day cards can mean sacrificing on the work or housekeeping fronts.

At the same time, we appreciate the importance of these traditions. They anchor us to our families' cultures. They give us a beautiful sense of continuity and connection. They bring us warmth and rekindle the love we have for our families, our lives, and the wonderful things we share. Plus, traditions bring us joy. It's a simple as that.

If, however, there is a tradition that does not bring you joy, one of the greatest gifts you can give yourself is to rethink it. People hate the idea of discarding holiday rituals, so I suggest something more temporary: this year, go without it, and see how that works for you. If your family always makes homemade fruitcake and spends hours and hundreds of dollars gathering ingredients, baking, and sending these cakes, then try a year without them. Tell people you are taking a sabbatical—or don't say a word. If, at the end of the season, you find that you've enjoyed a much freer, less-frazzled holiday, then it is a tradition that you're better off without. If, however, you find you really missed the tradition, circle back to it the next year, perhaps in a different, more streamlined way—for example, with a fruitcake-baking party that happens at your home or a local cooking space. Or, instead of making everyone a full-sized cake, halve the recipe and send everyone a mini loaf.

In making your celebrations easier, calmer, and more intimate, you are not only making them more enjoyable (and certainly more doable) for you and others, you are creating a deep sense of hygge. Paring down so you can focus on those activities you decide are worthy of keeping around is at the heart of hygge. Here are some additional ways to bring calm to special observances.

Limit contact with people who leave you in a negative place. You may not feel comfortable celebrating a holiday without your parents, but if you feel unsettled after seeing them, restrict your together time to no more than two hours. If your mother-in-law is difficult in groups, find a more private way to spend holiday time with her. If your roommate from college gets belligerent when she drinks, skip inviting her to your New Year's Eve cocktail party and instead see her for coffee in the New Year.

Get enough sleep. Everything you do—from thinking to rearranging furniture—will feel more difficult when you are tired. And every challenge and drama and stressor will seem to expand in huge ways when you are weary. For this reason, it is imperative you get enough sleep during times of holidays and celebrations. Make it a priority to get the sleep you need, be that seven and a half hours or nine hours or more. You will be delighted at how much easier and more pleasant your holidays will be when you are well rested.

Make a list. Write down everything that stresses you about holidays or special observances (such as birthdays and anniversaries). Your list may be a mile long or consist of just two or three items. It doesn't matter—you just want a clear idea of which activities are applying pressure. Because when it comes down to it, it isn't the occasion itself that causes stress; it's how you commemorate it that makes you feel unhinged.

Go down that list and downsize, downsize, downsize. Limit gift-giving to your immediate family. Put a financial cap on how much you all can spend on a gift. Give a staff gift instead of individual presents. Save the big dinner for Christmas Day and just do appetizers and antipasti on Christmas Eve. Make a family donation to a local charity in lieu of one night of Hanukkah gifts. Leave the Independence Day barbecue after an hour. Have your Thanksgiving meal catered. And so on.

Go down that list and delete, delete, delete. It's okay to say no to traditions that don't carry special meaning for you. Don't host the Memorial Day picnic if you've never enjoyed doing so. Don't send holiday cards. Don't feel you need to give gifts to every single person you know. Let someone else host the annual pumpkin carving contest—and the yearly Easter egg dyeing party, too. Tell your teens you're done hosting birthday parties for them and give them money to go to the movies with their friends. Just because your parents and grandparents scheduled a dozen activities around every single holiday, there's no rule that says that you have to do the same.

Ask for help. Maybe a May Day party sounds like good fun to you, but you just aren't up for cooking. You provide the backyard and the maypole and ask four or five of your best friends to bring the food. If you are hosting a get-together, be sure to ask each guest to bring something. You can do this gracefully by including this line on the invitation: "Please bring a dish of your choice to share! Thank you!"

Share your intentions. If the only thing stopping you from simplifying your celebrations is the fear of other people's opinions, be honest. Tell your friends and family members that you are looking for a new, simpler, deeper way to commemorate special occasions and that you look forward to celebrating with them in a more relaxed way. People will think you are brilliant!

*"The less there is to justify a traditional custom,
the harder it is to get rid of it."*

—Mark Twain

TAP INTO THE MAGIC OF IMPROMPTU CELEBRATIONS

Throughout this book, we've focused on the importance of togetherness in creating a cozy, hygge-inspired life. This means setting up your schedule, home, and life so that you're ready for anything, from a movie night with the kids to an impromptu coffee hour with neighbors. This "ready to go" attitude is especially liberating during the holidays. Instead of bemoaning all the things you need to do in order to celebrate a holiday, you can just relax and get on with the celebrating—even if that celebrating happens to be last-minute in nature. (Because, let's face it, some of the best kinds of celebrations are those we throw together at the spur of the moment.)

Said another way, when you have time to relax and your home is warm and free of clutter and grime, it is easy to enjoy surprise Halloween visitors or indulge in a last-minute desire to host a New Year's Day brunch for your neighbors.

One of the things I like to have on hand to make it even easier to indulge my desires for spontaneous festivities is a celebration box. In my case, this is an old wooden box that once held a case of Malbec from Chile. I keep it on a high shelf in my hallway closet. It contains:

- A few CDs of classical music that is just exciting enough to create an atmosphere without inducing slumber. You can also create a quick "company's coming" playlist to instantly access next time unexpected guests arrive.

- A collection of small soy-based or beeswax votive candles and a lighter. I adore scented candles, but I am aware that these can set off asthma or other respiratory conditions in some people, so I go for soy-based unscented candles.

I place one in each bathroom, one in the dining room, and one in each of the four corners of my living room. Then I dim the lights to create comfortable warmth.

- A few throws to toss on the sofa if there is a stain that needs to be covered.

- A bottle of wine. Putting one up on a high shelf ensures that my husband and I save it for company.

- A bag of pistachios in the shell—the ultimate highbrow snack—and two small, pretty bowls, one for the pistachios and one for the shells.

It may sound silly, but having a few party supplies tucked away makes it simple to upgrade a social visit to a special occasion. Putting a celebration box together takes no time at all, meaning it is something you can do today. What will you put in your box?

TAKING THE CELEBRATION OUTSIDE

Many of the observances we celebrate center around hearth and home. And yet, if you think back to your childhood, I bet there are a host of outdoor events that you lovingly remember even today. From beachside clambakes to Independence Day picnics at the city park, from parking lot tailgate parties to family reunion barbecues, outdoor gatherings are easy and fun, and they create such happiness and good memories. My Danish family is brilliant at outdoor entertaining, from simple porch visits with the aunties to wild asparagus-gathering expeditions, giving us a deep connection to the land and to one another. Even though I live in a New York City apartment with no yard, I make it a point to have three outdoor gatherings a year. Need some ideas for outdoor amusements? Try one (or more) of these:

Head to the water. Danes adore water. Lakes, beaches, pools— wherever there is water in Denmark, there is a collection of people on beach chairs, faces turned to the sun, soaking up the rays. Those of us here in the States like water just as much, which is why you can't go wrong by sending out an email asking friends to meet you at the local public pool or a nearby beach. Bring some outdoor games and a few balls so you can enjoy some group exercise.

Host a backyard party. If you're lucky enough to have a yard, outdoor entertaining is a no-brainer. Invite several families over for an outdoor potluck. Put out some folding chairs and supply a stack of picnic blankets, set up a buffet table with disposable tableware, and ask each family to bring a few dishes. Then simply hang out and visit. There's no need to try to create a theme for your event or come up with children's entertainment; being together is enough.

Throw a barbecue. Everyone loves a barbecue. If you live in the 'burbs, your backyard is the perfect place. You grill the main dishes, ask your friends to bring drinks, side dishes, and marshmallows to roast over the barbecue for dessert. If you don't have private outdoor space, most cities have parks or nearby state (or even national) parks with public-use grills. Host your party there.

Gather on your front porch. Ask two or three of your closest friends to come over for lemonade and gossip on your front porch. Want to include an activity? Try hosting summer knitting, needlework, or jigsaw puzzle nights on your porch.

Go picking or gathering. One of my favorite childhood activities was picking fruit. We didn't have a lot of money growing up, so several times each year, my parents and one or two other families would travel to secret spots where we would pick wild berries, plums, tomatoes, or herbs. We'd take a picnic lunch and make it a social outing. With my father's aunts, we often would go hunting for wild asparagus, which grew in the apple orchards around their homes. Now that I am a mom, in the summer my kids and I pick berries and stone fruit. In the autumn it is apples, pears, and pumpkins.

Make a party out of good deeds. When I was growing up, my Sunday school teacher would organize charity work for us around Thanksgiving to show us how much we had to be thankful for. This outdoor work usually consisted of cleaning up a public area and taking items to a recycling center (the money we earned was donated to charity). We had so much fun that my church friends and I looked forward to this activity each year. What outdoor charity work you can do? Clean up a stretch of road? Paint park benches? Help out at a local campground? Look for opportunities for your family and friends to get involved in a meaningful cause while enjoying the great outdoors.

Tailgate. Tailgating is something everyone should do at least once in his or her life. I don't know if it's the food and drinks, the good company, or the pregame excitement, but there is something uniquely American about hanging out in a parking lot waiting for a game, concert, or other event to start. If there are no established tailgate parties in your community, organize one yourself. You can enjoy one before a big high school game, a youth soccer game, or a university playoff match.

Bundle up. Many of us confine our outdoor gatherings to warm-weather activities. Danes, however, find a way to bring hygge even to winter. Bundle up, fill a few thermoses with hot cider or cocoa, and head out to an outdoor ice skating rink for a few hours of one of Scandinavia's favorite activities. Other cold-weather Danish favorites that you're sure to love include old-fashioned snow-people-making contests, snowball fights, or even gathering together to clear snow from a group of homes. Or if snow isn't your thing, get out the bicycles and take a winter bike ride through town. Invite everyone inside when you're finished so they can warm up in front of the fire. A glass of glogg (see the recipe on page 132) can help unthaw everyone quickly and deliciously.

GLOGG: LIQUID HYGGE

Glogg is a warmed, spiced wine, enjoyed during the winter holidays in Denmark. Feel free to double the recipe if you'd like.

MAKES 4 SERVINGS

- ¹/₂ cup honey
- 5 whole cloves
- 2 cardamom pods
- 2 cinnamon sticks
- ¹/₂ cup orange juice
- Rind of 1 orange
- 1 cup raisins
- 1 bottle (750 milliliters) full-bodied red wine, such as Syrah or Malbec (drinkable, but not expensive)

1. Add the honey, cloves, cardamom, cinnamon, orange juice, orange rind, and 1 cup of water to a large pot over medium-high heat. Bring to a boil, and then reduce the heat and simmer for 30 minutes.

2. Remove the spices and rind from the liquid.

3. Add the raisins and the bottle of wine to the spiced liquid.

4. Turn the heat up to medium-high and bring to a gentle simmer. Allow to simmer for 5 minutes.

5. Turn off the heat.

6. Ladle into mugs. Include a spoon, if desired, so people can enjoy the glogg-soaked raisins.

Special occasions take on a deeply meaningful quality when you remove elements that cause you stress or do not honor your priorities. It may take a level of bravery on your part to forgo tradition and do something different, but please give yourself the gift of at least one holiday season without those traditions that leave you feeling more tired, overspent, and irritable than happy, inspired, and grateful. I can say with confidence that removing actions that you resent or that you see as burdens allow you to delve delightfully deep into the pursuits that you do commit to keeping in your life. In other words: by removing what does not serve you, you have no choice but to focus completely on the traditions you feel are most important. This is hygge.

CHAPTER EIGHT

COZY SCHEDULES: MULTITASKING AND OTHER COMFORT KILLERS

I t is impossible to have a comfortable life if your days are cluttered with too many tasks, too much busywork, and excessive screen time. These time fillers can clutter your days and leave you feeling rushed, anxious, brain-dead, and numb. Not a cozy way to approach life, is it?

Many of us thrive on go-go-going. It's important to get a lot done. Further, since there are only 24 hours in a day—and at least 10 of them are spent sleeping and eating—there is no way to fit all of our activities into the remaining 14 hours if we do not multitask.

If you're rushing through this chapter, trying to ignore the possibility that cramming too much into your day could be causing stress—or at least making life a whole lot less comfy than it could be—then you, more than anyone, will benefit from what you will find here.

"Things which matter most must never be at the mercy of things which matter least."

—Johann Wolfgang von Goethe

WHY SIMPLIFYING YOUR LIFE IS SO DIFFICULT

Burnt out, overscheduled, overextended, crazed, insane—if you use these words regularly to describe your life, let me ask: Are you looking for a badge of honor for cramming more into your life? If you suddenly could perform only one task a day, how would you describe your life to others? Do you connect being overly busy with competence or success?

If so, you're not alone. For many people, multitasking defines them. It makes them look (or so they think) unusually efficient to whomever is paying attention and gives a sense of purpose to their lives.

Our parents didn't do much more than we did. They left for work, and then came home. Or, they just stayed at home. Leisure time was some post-dinner television or sitting out on the front porch with neighbors doing nothing but talking. No phones, televisions, or laptops pulled focus away from the conversation.

My point is that there were no social kudos for doing more than anyone else. Our parents couldn't jump on social media with pictures from their kid's travel soccer team tournament or post humblebrags claiming gratitude for pulling off a particularly challenging weekend of juggling three work projects, a home renovation, and running a marathon. There was no adoring audience ready to cheer them every time they boasted about being overextended—not that they ever thought being overwhelmed was something to toot their horns about.

Beyond the social credibility we currently think we attain by pulling off a lot of activity in a small amount of time, there is an addictive rush of adrenaline that comes with being overextended. However, research has shown that when humans multitask—such as finishing a work project while sending emails, or cooking dinner while texting—we get less work done, work more slowly, and perform at a lower level than when we simply focus on a single task at a time.

The bottom line is that stuffing our day with activities and then layering constant emailing, texting, calling, and web surfing on top of those undertakings can leave us feeling temporarily accomplished in the short run. What being overextended does over time is not so enjoyable, however, and can directly affect our ability to create and enjoy a calm, centered life.

COULD YOUR PHONE BE THE PROBLEM?

Could your phone responsible for the lack of time in your day? Check out these statistics regarding just how often we focus on our screens.

- According to data collected on 15,000 people by the New York–based app maker Locket, the average person unlocks his or her phone 110 times a day.

- The 2013 Internet Trends Report by venture capital firm Kleiner Perkins Caufield and Byers (KPCB) found that the average user checks their phone nearer to 150 times per day.

- Three years later, KPCB's "Internet Trends 2017" report found that people spend an average of 3.1 hours accessing the internet from their phones—that's not even counting texting, emailing, or making video or voice phone calls.

- A 2015 survey of 2,000 people by tech protection company Asurion found that one in 10 people check their phones on average once every four minutes, and the majority cannot go 10 minutes without sneaking a peek.

THE POWER OF SINGLE-TASKING AND SIMPLE LIVING

If you have never heard of the term *single-tasking*, it means—literally—to attend to a single task at a time. Make the bed, then call your mother, then get dressed for work, then drive to the office, and so on. Humans have lived successfully for millions of years doing one thing at a time. Sure, there are small exceptions here and there—your son calls right as you're feeding the cat, or you are chatting with your husband as you toss a load of laundry into the dryer, for instance—but the human nervous system is healthiest when it can dig in and really work on a single task.

The two biggest roadblocks to single-tasking are an addiction to doing more than one thing at a time, and a schedule so overstuffed with activity that the only way to fit everything in is to double-book yourself and juggle various tasks.

Let's talk about that first belief. If you don't believe just how healthy it can be to ditch the multitasking, consider the following studies.

Multitasking is less productive than doing one thing at a time.
Researchers at Stanford University led 100 students through three tests to learn the dangers or benefits of multitasking. One test gauged the ability to focus while ignoring distractions, the second measured how memory was affected by multitasking, and the third determined how fast the brain can switch back and forth between tasks. On every test, the multitaskers did worse than the single-taskers. The unsettling results were published in the August 24, 2009, edition of the *Proceedings of the National Academy of Sciences.*

Excuse me, you just dropped your IQ. A 2015 study at the University of London found that participants who multitasked during cognitive tasks experienced declines in IQ scores that were similar to what they'd expect if they had smoked marijuana or stayed up all night. IQ drops of 15 points for multitasking men lowered their scores to the average range of an eight-year-old child.

Multitasking can distract you, even when you're not currently multitasking! In the University of London study mentioned above, it was discovered that just knowing an unread email was sitting in their inbox was so distracting to multitaskers that their IQs dropped by 10 points.

Multitasking may damage your brain. In 2014, a team of researchers from the University of Sussex used MRI technology to look at the brains of 40 individuals who regularly used two or more forms of media (watching television, answering emails, talking on the phone, and so on) while simultaneously completing tasks. MRIs of these individuals showed that they had less gray matter in a region called the anterior cingulate cortex (ACC) than individuals who did not multitask. The ACC is the part of the brain that is involved in processing emotion and is associated with memory and concentration.

Doing one thing at a time isn't necessarily doing *less*; it is doing *better*. Danes know that we only have so much time in a day, and honoring each of these moments—even those spent working or doing chores—with your attention is an easy way to be more present and live in the moment. Even if you don't agree with me, I urge you to try single-tasking for a month to see how your life can change. The benefits to living this way are feelings of groundedness, peace, and well-being that leave you feeling as if you can do anything.

IDEAS FOR SINGLE-TASKING

To wrap your head around the very Danish idea of one thing at a time, here are some hygge-inspired activities you can incorporate into your weekday.

- Exercise—without a phone or screen.

- Pray, meditate, or just sit and look out the window.

- Take time in the morning to prepare for your day. Turn on the teakettle; put some beans, brown rice, or ingredients for bone broth in the slow cooker; put laundry in the wash.

- Have a (phone-free) breakfast with your partner or kids.

- Take your dog for a walk.

- Walk your child to or from school if possible. This gives you time to talk and is great exercise.

- Leave the office for lunch. Listen to music, go to a park, or sit in a local hotel lobby or coffee shop.

- Stay connected. Chat with other parents when picking up kids from school, and set aside time for making or returning phone calls from friends.

- Go to bed with a book, notepad, and pen (not a screen) for reading or writing.

AVOIDING BURNOUT

My own overscheduling epiphany came, perhaps not so strangely, with something called burnout. I woke up one day and had a strong aversion to social media. When a friend sent a link to a funny post that she knew I hadn't seen, I ignored it. Days later, when another friend urged me on Facebook to watch a clip, I panicked. Soon, checking my email messages became so scary that I did everything I could to avoid it.

As my burnout grew, so did the number of activities I began avoiding, from going to church to hear my sons sing to working with clients. My sleep became disrupted and I developed a general apathy about my sons' schoolwork, walking the dog, and grocery shopping.

On a whim, I took a friend's suggestion to read a book on simplifying my life. Then I read another. And another. I am not saying changing your life is as simple as reading a book, but in reading what others had to say on the topic, I came away with new beliefs around productivity and efficiency. The following tips worked especially well for me as I identified and addressed the frenzy that lead to my burnout.

Humans work differently than computers and smartphones do.
Our brains solve a problem and then move to the next task, happily ready to conquer the new challenge. Computers and smartphones are just fine pulling up new sites when 10 tabs are already open. Your beautiful human brain is built differently than a computer motherboard. There is nothing wrong with a human brain that behaves like a human brain. Stop judging yourself for failing to take on—and complete—a machine-sized mountain of work in a human's time frame.

Playing to your humanness helps make life calmer. Act like a human and not an automaton, computer, or some multitasking bot. Humans enjoy focusing on one thing, putting it away, and then working on something else, putting it away, and moving on to something else. There are times when one must multitask (more on that in a bit), such as texting your husband while walking the dog, but the less multitasking you do, the easier it is to complete what you want to complete in the time in which you want to complete it, without hurting your mental health.

Get clear on any benefits you may be receiving from keeping life so busy. Is there a reason you've chosen to live such a packed life? According to Elaine St. James, author of *Living the Simple Life*, part of why we overstuff our lives is "so we won't have to listen to our inner voice telling us what we need to do to make our lives work better." What is your inner voice telling you? What are you avoiding?

What would your ideal schedule look like? What can you get rid of, outsource, or do differently to move toward your ideal?

Simplifying my life was exactly the hygge I grew up with—a form of moment-to-moment mindfulness so natural that it has shaped generations of Scandinavians. There is nothing odd or exotic or complicated about it. It is the simple act of focusing on something and lavishing it with your attention, whether it is cleaning up mashed sweet potatoes from a baby's face or reading an amusing text from your hilarious best friend.

WHAT IS BURNOUT?

Burnout is a state of emotional, mental, and physical exhaustion caused by chronic—aka prolonged—stress. Burnout develops over time and occurs when you feel overwhelmed, emotionally drained, and unable to meet constant demands in your life. There is a perception that burnout is caused by excessive work or school demands, but in truth, any part of your life can contribute to feeling "burned out," including your emotional life, your parenting life, romantic or extended family relationships, managing illness, or financial concerns.

While mental health experts don't agree on the exact signs of burnout, the following are generally accepted as warning signs.

- Physical and emotional exhaustion. One of the first signs of burnout is a lack of physical, emotional, and mental energy,

as well as insomnia. Impaired concentration, forgetfulness, lowered immune system function, loss of appetite, anxiety, anger, and even depression can also develop.

- Feelings of ineffectiveness and lack of accomplishment. A "why bother?" attitude overtakes you, and it seems like nothing you do really matters. You may find that you no longer can work as quickly or for as long as you once did and tasks that were once easy for you seem overwhelmingly complicated. It may seem as if no matter how hard you try, you never complete your daily to-do list.

- Cynicism and detachment. You may find that you simply don't enjoy life anymore. You move through your days on automatic pilot, all glasses appear half empty, and you begin to isolate yourself from other people as you grow wary that they will ask you to do something for them.

If left unchecked, burnout can damage not only your mental health but your physical health as well. If you suspect that you are in the throes of burnout, consider making an appointment with your mental health or medical health provider, and read this chapter for ideas on combating it.

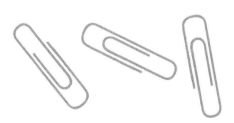

PARING DOWN WITHOUT ANGST

If you are excited by the idea of stripping your daily to-do list to the most important tasks but worry you won't be able to keep up at work, take care of your family, or maintain your household by doing less than you do now, don't despair. Giving up a few of your behaviors, tendencies, and habits can open up wonderful pockets of time—while ridding your life of unwanted angst or irritations. Here are some ideas.

Find time to enjoy calm. You are busy—so busy you may be wondering how in the world you can enjoy that cozy feeling of hygge in your frenzied life. It helps to find hidden pockets of time to relax. Think about the waiting you do each day (commuting, standing in checkout lines, and so on) and your "official" breaks (your lunch hour). Instead of texting your way through them or using this bonus time to pay bills, check stock prices, or hop on social media, give yourself the meditative opportunity to breathe deeply and empty your mind. Even a 30-second meditation break here and there will lower your heart rate and leave you feeling grounded and at peace, making you more focused, happier, and less reactive.

Calm begets calm. If you've ever met a Dane, you know they are seemingly unflappable. Danes have as much to do each day as you do, but they carry calm with them wherever they go. This sense of calm is an important element of hygge. It is also something you can create for yourself with an easy mindset trick: don't think too much. The more deeply you analyze your daily tasks, the more stressed you may become. Commit to completing the tasks on your to-do list without getting emotionally invested.

Look at the "reactionary activities" in your life. These are time-sucking activities created by the actions of others, such as listening to a friend complain about her son's school, or picking up someone else's wet towels from the floor. How can you remove these activities from your life? Or at least lessen the time you spend on them?

Celebrate the interactions you have with other people. How can you use the time spent together as a way for deep connection? Do you walk your daughter to or from school each day? Use this time not to check your email but to ask her questions about her life or answer her queries. Use this travel time as an opportunity to deepen your relationship.

Create a dedicated email answering time. Most email providers allow you to program an automatic reply that is immediately sent to anyone who emails you. Program your personal emails to say "Hello! Thank you for contacting me! I answer emails from 7 to 8:30 p.m., Monday through Friday. I will reply to you then. Be well!" A wonderful side benefit to using an auto-reply message is it makes it easier to decline unwanted invitations or say no to people or activities that don't serve you. At work, talk to your supervisor about choosing two or three times during the workday when you can check and respond to messages.

Limit your extracurricular activities. Decide how many weekly activities are enough. For extroverts, this could be three or four. For introverts, perhaps it's one or two. Once you've hit upon your number, it's time to quit: if you've already agreed to a cocktail party and a night at the ballet, decline all other invitations for that week. You are allowing yourself only a fixed number of nights out, which means you get to be selective and choose only those activities that excite you.

Schedule nightly and morning downtime. Fifteen or 30 private minutes before bed and upon waking—or longer, if you are able to dedicate more time to yourself—is a wonderful gift to give yourself. Use this time to do whatever you'd like, from staring out the window with a cup of tea, to a bubble bath, to meditation. When we are generous with ourselves, we are less likely to stray off course during the day looking for opportunities for "me time," which may show up in surfing shopping sites, checking social media on your phone, getting involved in a gossipy text thread that doesn't uplift you, or some other low-quality activity that sucks up your time.

Schedule time for exercise. Our bodies are made to move. Daily sustained movement of 20 minutes or more helps your body maintain a healthy weight, keeps muscles (including your heart) strong, creates a feeling of calm energy, and boosts mental acuity and focus—all of which will make it more joyful and effortless to start and finish your daily tasks. Walking, cycling, yoga, dancing, rowing, some gym time—it doesn't matter what you choose, as long as your body is moving.

A life filled with space and purpose feels different than a life over-stuffed with obligations and mindless activity. Sure, switching to a more hygge-friendly schedule will not completely erase those chores you don't love, but by removing the noisy, stress-creating emotional clutter, your life will feel suddenly feel exciting and fulfilling. Try it and see.

CHAPTER NINE

COZY BUSINESS:
YOUR WORK LIFE, HYGGEIFIED

One of the biggest differences I see between my American friends and my Danish friends is how much time they spend working. I'm basing this on observation: My Danish friends get to work between 8 and 9 a.m. They work hard, and then, at 4:45 p.m., they begin packing up. By 5 p.m., they're out the door and do not think about or do anything work related (including checking and answering emails) until the next day when they are at their desks. They allow themselves to stroll home, hang out with family, take a guitar lesson or a yoga class, or do whatever it is they want to do with their non-work time.

Research backs me up. According to 2016 figures from the Organisation for Economic Co-operation and Development, Danes who are employed full-time work an average of 32.1 hours a week; full-time employees who live in the US work an average of 38.6 hours a week. (A 2014 Gallup poll found that full-time workers in the US work an average of 47 hours per week, which includes late nights at the office and using weekend time for "job work.")

At its foundation, creating a work-life balance is about boundaries. If you've ever known any Danes, you know how strong their boundaries are—around everything from personal beliefs to what they will or won't do and when they will or won't do it. "Sure," you might say. "It's easy for them. Here in the States, we are expected to work until we drop. For the Danes, moderation is built into the culture."

You would be right. But a revolution must start somewhere, so why not here, right now, with this chapter? By moving from quantity of work to quality of work, you gain more hours in each day—that's more hours to spend with yourself, to be in reflection, to stop and smell the roses, to read a book to a child, to help a neighbor in need, to take a nap, to take your dog out for a long walk, to invite friends over for tea, or to just snuggle on the sofa and celebrate how lucky you are. All of these are important components of your cozy life.

THE CONNECTION BETWEEN
WORK AND STRESS

Anyone who has ever worked knows there is a connection between your work life and your health. Studies back this up.

- In 2012, 65 percent of Americans cited work as a top source of stress, according to the American Psychological Association's annual "Stress in America" survey.

- A 2013 survey by the American Psychological Association found that one-third of working Americans reported experiencing chronic work stress, and just 36 percent said their organizations provide sufficient resources to help them manage that stress.

- Scientists at Ohio State University say that job satisfaction in your early career plays a major role in your long-term health. Just a decade or so after landing that crummy job, you could have trouble sleeping, grapple with mental health issues, and face back pain or chronic colds more often than your peers who started their careers on a happy note.

- In a long-term study by researchers at Ohio State University, it was found that low job satisfaction may cause depression or cardiovascular disease years later.

It is clear that, for many individuals, modern work is deeply unhealthy. If you feel defeated and depressed by your work, read this chapter and seek help if necessary. Life is a beautiful gift. We work to support this gift. We don't live to work, but work to live.

THE LEISURE–PRODUCTIVITY CONNECTION

Once upon a time, I was under the mistaken belief that working long hours must translate to earning a high income. But as I watched my friends who worked shorter days—some from countries like Denmark or France, where companies are forbidden to send their employees work emails after 5 p.m.—I realized that the number of hours spent in an office has very little to do with a person's productivity. These friends were more relaxed, cheerful, and focused than me and the rest of us bleary-eyed workers who dragged ourselves to work at 8 a.m., worked through our lunch hours, and were slogging away at the computer well after 7 p.m.

As I studied how different countries around the world approach productivity, I was surprised to find that—for the most part—the countries that worked the most were not the countries that were generating the most money. And vice versa. For some numbers that directly support this chapter's emphasis about creating a rich, cozy life by reining in your work hours, check out these average numbers from 2016 data collected by the Organisation for Economic Co-operation and Development (all dollar amounts are given in US dollars).

- In Luxembourg, people work an average of 37.3 hours per week. For every hour a person works, $93.7 per hour is generated.

- In Germany, people work, on average, a bit more than 34 hours a week. For every hour a person works, $68 per hour is generated.

- In the United States, people work an average of 38.6 hours a week. For every hour worked in the US, a little over $69 per hour is generated per person.

- In Denmark, people work an average of 32.1 hours per week, generating $69.7 per hour per person. Denmark is not that much behind the United States, even though the country's citizens spend less time at the workplace.

- In Portugal, people work 39.4 hours per week. For every hour a person works, a little over $36 per hour is generated.

- In Korea, people work an average of 43.7 hours per week. For every hour a person works, just over $34 per hour is generated.

- In Mexico, people work an average of 45.2 hours per week. For every hour a person works, a little under $20 per hour is generated.

If you're a numbers person, you'll notice that there is a correlation between more leisure time and higher productivity, as well as the reverse: less leisure time can mean less productivity.

*"It is better to rise from life as from a banquet—
neither thirsty nor drunken."*

—Aristotle

CREATING A BOUNDARY AROUND YOUR PERSONAL LIFE

A boundary is like a fence, which shows where one thing ends and another begins. But a boundary isn't always a physical barrier. For many of us, the most important boundaries we'll ever encounter are the limits we must create to protect ourselves from the energy-sucking people and time-stealing activities that encroach on our personal lives. These comfort thieves can be overtime work, requests from others, addiction to electronic devices, clutter, and anything else that erodes the spacious expanse of time we need to live a calm, meaningful, cozy life—in other words, to enjoy our own brand of hygge.

If any of this is striking a chord with you, you already know that a PTA bake sale request often comes at the very same time you have a big sales report due, or a plumbing emergency appears as you are trying to refinance your mortgage or manage any other constellation of minor emergencies. Often we try to address one or two of these distractions immediately. The remaining are brought home to tackle on our personal time.

If you're looking to create a more comfortable, cozier life, the simplest piece of work advice you can follow is this: be clear about how much non-work time you want each day, and then create boundaries around those hours, separating them from your work life. By saying no to working past a certain point each day (or working on weekends or holidays), you can enjoy dinner with your children, an important conversation with your partner, the sleep you deserve, and more. If you're frightened by the thought of saying no to your employer or giving up the possibility of paying work, then look at this from a different angle: you can only say yes to one thing at a time. Anything that is not a yes is a no. By saying yes to your boss's request to work overtime, you've said no to a comfy, cozy night of connection with your family (or quality time with yourself).

If leaving the office by 6 p.m. sounds like your idea of heaven, then start taking steps to make it happen, by being efficient, effective, and productive during your work hours. Being effective at work means you stop spending time chatting at the watercooler, nix the multiple mochaccino runs, and avoid wandering over to social media. It can help to send a wrap-up email each evening before you leave, listing what you've completed, what you're currently working on, any due dates coming up, and so on. This lets your supervisors know you are engaged, productive, and on top of your work.

I challenge you to try it for a week and see what happens. By focusing exclusively on your work during business hours, you may be surprised to find that you able to get as much done by 6 p.m. as you formerly did by 8:30 p.m.

The second part of this experiment centers on what you do when you leave your work—or, more importantly, what you *don't* do. Do not answer work emails, texts, or calls. Talking, calling, emailing, or texting about work is the same as working after hours. If this worries you, set your email with an autoreply that says, "Hello! Thanks for contacting me. I will be in the office tomorrow at 9 a.m."

For those of you who are freelancers or entrepreneurs, this applies to you as well. In fact, if your office is in the same space as your home, you will need to be even more vigilant about creating impenetrable boundaries between your work life and your personal life. By working efficiently during your designated business hours, you can feel calm and at peace stepping away at the end of each day.

"Don't confuse having a career with having a life."

—Hillary Clinton

FIVE THOUSAND EMAILS ARE TOO MANY

Setting boundaries between your work and personal life is one of the most important steps you can take to reclaiming your happiness, your personal energy, and your sense of peace. But there are also steps you can take at work to increase your professional well-being while making your 9-to-5 infinitely more enjoyable than it is now. Here are some tips to hyggeify your work life.

Get rid of electronic clutter. Clean out each of your email folders, including your inbox, sent, draft, and junk folders. A recent study performed by the Radicati Group, a market research firm, showed that the average person receives 121 work emails a day. All clutter takes up a certain amount of psychological space. Find a regular system for decluttering your email files, such as spending five minutes at the end of each day deleting things, or earmarking a Saturday morning each month for cleaning out already-read emails, spam, and promotional newsletters.

Clean up your computer desktop. A desktop cluttered with photos, file icons, and other material looks sloppy—and can make you feel the same way. A clean desktop leaves you feeling calm and refreshed and ensures you're not scrambling through visual clutter to find a needed file.

Don't forget your hard drive. The more files that are on your drive, the longer it takes your computer to finish a task, the more likely it is to freeze or get stuck, and the harder it is for you to work efficiently. Delete items as they become obsolete, and spend a few minutes each evening getting rid of things you don't need.

Place a plant on your desk. Studies have proven that indoor plants improve concentration and productivity, reduce stress levels, and boost your mood, as well as remove indoor air pollution and add humidity to dry air. Visit a nursery and ask for help choosing a plant that will do well in your particular office environment. For instance, if you're in a windowless space with fluorescent lighting, oxalis, jade plants, umbrella plants, peace lilies, bamboo, and English ivy are great options.

Spruce up your desk with flowers. Have you ever wondered why flowers make you feel happy? According to behavioral research conducted at Rutgers University, people reported feeling less depressed, anxious, and agitated after receiving flowers, and demonstrated a higher sense of enjoyment and life satisfaction when in the presence of flowers.

Go bright! Many modern workspaces are lit by fluorescent lighting. It's relatively cheap and produces a lot of light. And it may also leave you feeling sluggish, according to several studies. Researchers at Korea Advanced Institute of Science and Technology studied 54 fourth-grade test takers. One group was in a room lit with florescent lights, and the other in a room equipped with LED lights that mimicked natural daylight. Students in the fluorescent light group were less alert and performed less well on the exam than the other group. While you cannot get rid of your employer's fluorescent lights, you can place a small lamp with a daylight bulb on your desk.

Clear away clutter. Many studies on clutter have found that it decreases your efficiency, dampens your motivation, adds time to your ability to finish a task, makes it difficult for you to focus, leads to irritability, and makes it hard for you to process information. Think how much faster you could tackle work assignments (meaning you could leave work on time) if you could focus more fully. Spend a few minutes at the end of each day organizing your desk, and earmark 30 minutes each Friday for a deeper clean. And never, ever use your cubicle or office as storage space for personal, non-work items.

Get comfortable. If your desk chair is uncomfortable or in poor shape, ask for a replacement. We spend about five and a half hours each workday sitting, according to researchers at the British Psychological Society. If your chair leaves your back hurting or your leg cramped, or if you are constantly squirming to find comfort, you may need a new chair. If your company doesn't have a few spare chairs for you to try out, consider using your own money to buy a chair that feels great. Look for an ergonomic model, made to support the human body. If the thought of spending your own money on a fancy office chair seems crazy to you, consider this: spending money to keep your body healthy and your brain productive is worthwhile. Plus, you can take the chair with you if you move to another company.

Hang a framed inspirational quote. Affirmations are a popular tool in the self-actualization world, reminding us that thoughts become things. Do they work? Research is mixed, but if reminding you to keep calm and carry on helps you to do just that, then hang away.

Get up and move once an hour. Movement will help your circulation, sending oxygen-rich blood to your brain and body, which in turn will energize you and help you focus. At a certain time every hour, stand and take a quick walk around the office. You can also step into the stairwell and climb a few flights or go down to the street and walk quickly around the block.

Do not eat lunch at your desk. Get in the habit of going somewhere else for lunch. The change of scenery will help your productivity, and you'll have an opportunity to socialize with coworkers, go outdoors, or do something pleasant, giving you a mini break from work. You'll feel refreshed and focused when you're ready to return to your desk.

If you sit near someone who makes it difficult for you to focus, ask to move. At one magazine I worked at, I was stationed near two ad salesmen who were constantly on the phone. While that made it difficult for me to write, the real problem was that many of their discussions had nothing to do with ad sales. These men were constantly sharing intimate details of their personal lives. When I finally got brave enough to ask my employer for a new cubicle, his first response was no. I persisted, was honest about why, and got my wish. You'll be more productive when you are not distracted.

TRADE DRAMA FOR CURIOSITY

Success is often less about what you do and more about what you think. Take a minute to consider your attitude toward your work. Are you someone who needs a lot of pushing to get a project started? Do you, on some level, love work drama? Maybe you are a complainer or have something else going on with your relationship to work. Whatever it is, make a mental note of your feelings around work and your workplace.

Work takes up an enormous amount of our days—of our lives. If you are spending hours each day sitting in a swamp of negative emotions, you're not going to feel much coziness, calm, or contentment in your life.

You don't have to love what you do, but if you can approach each project, each coworker, and each workday with a sense of genuine curiosity, you will quickly feel a change in your life. There is something magical—a hygge-creating lightness and openness—about curiosity.

It is difficult to be angry, resentful, superior, or frustrated when you are curious. Ask yourself: Why does your boss have images of llamas throughout her office? Why did the company choose this office building? If you don't believe that your work life can completely change by becoming curious about the things and people around you and the tasks you're asked to complete, I offer you an easy challenge. For one week, be curious about everyone, everything, and every assignment that you encounter in your work life. At the end of the week, if you don't feel a sense of peace around your job, then feel free to go back to what you were originally thinking, doing, and feeling. I am sure, however, you'll see a wonderful change in how you view your workday.

> *"Curiosity is, in great and generous minds,*
> *the first passion and the last."*
>
> —Samuel Johnson

ARE YOU AND YOUR JOB COMPATIBLE?

There are so many reasons people don't like their jobs, from having a tyrant of a supervisor, to poor workplace communication, to too much to do in too little time.

Being curious about the things around you is a very Danish way to approach life. It provides a sense of peace, no matter where you are and what you are doing. But what if you are curious about everything you come across each workday, and you still have this nagging feeling that your job is dragging you down?

Danes believe that your life is more important than your work. So, if your feelings about your work are negatively affecting your personal life, a job change may be in order. There are any number of life-coaching quizzes to help you decide if you and your current position are compatible. However, in my opinion, the only measure that really matters is your gut. If you feel that the job you are currently in is not the right one for you, you have an obligation to your soul to find the one that is.

Let me put that another way: happiness, comfort, coziness, contentment, peace—these beautiful states are not random or accidental. The perfect job will not just happen to you. Make your current position as good as possible. If you know in your gut you still need to move on, then begin taking steps to do that. The goodwill that you are now creating with your curiosity and positive, calm outlook will pave the way, opening doors for a more appropriate position.

In a Dane's mind, work and life are two separate things. You do one to be able to enjoy the other. While that may seem easier said than done, working efficiently, making your work life as pleasant as possible, and creating strong boundaries between the two is one of the Danish secrets of hygge. Keep your work life from spilling into your personal life so you can luxuriate in the coziness of your home life.

CHAPTER TEN

COZY STYLE:
SIMPLY LOOKING YOUR BEST

What are your thoughts around the way you look? Do you spend a lot of time thinking about what to wear, applying cosmetics, shopping for hair-care products, or hanging and organizing your clothes? For many of us, cultivating and caring for our appearance is one of the most time-consuming, expensive, and frustrating parts of our day. Fortunately, nurturing your looks doesn't have to mean hours spent hunting for new potions or the latest trendy wardrobe piece. As you'll see here, focusing on a more minimalist approach can allow your unique beauty to shine bright.

COSMETICS FACTS

Here are some statistics that underscore just how much we focus on our looks.

- The online beauty store SkinStore recently surveyed 3,000 of its American shoppers on skin-care and cosmetic use. The survey found that women in New York spend about $300,000 just on their face (in the form of skin-care products and makeup) during their lifetimes.

- This same survey found that 85 percent of the women surveyed applied a minimum of 16 products to their face before leaving the house each day, from facial cleansers to cosmetics.

- Data published by finance site Mint.com found that between the ages of 16 and 65, the average American woman spends $15,000 on makeup—$3,770 of that on mascara, $2,750 on eye shadow, and $1,780 on lipstick.

- According to data from *Money* magazine, an American woman spends an average of $43 each time she shops for makeup.

WARDROBE FACTS

Choosing what to wear is also a big part of our day. Take a look at these facts.

- A poll of 2,000 people by Marks & Spencer, a major UK retailer, found that the average woman spends 17 minutes each weekday picking out what to wear. (That comes out to four full days every year, or six solid months between high school graduation and retirement!)

- One in 10 adults surveyed admitted to regularly arriving late to work because it took them so long to choose the day's outfit. One in 20 actually missed an entire occasion because they took so long deciding what to wear.

- One in 20 survey respondents had 50 or more items in their closets with the tags still on. One in eight owned more than 300 items of clothing.

- The market research company OnePoll surveyed 2,000 American women and found that, on average, a woman spends more than 100 hours each year on 30 trips to shop for clothes. Shoes take about 15 shopping excursions, equaling 40 hours. And then there is the matter of window-shopping: women spend 50 hours a year just looking at clothing and shoes.

Take a moment to think about your relationship with your grooming routine and your wardrobe. There's a chance that these statistics aren't so different than the amount of time and money you spend on yourself.

BUT I'M WORTH IT!

Spending time and money on yourself isn't necessarily a bad thing. But for many of us, our quest to look a certain way is distracting enough to undermine our ability to live a calm, comfortable, cozy life.

Before I dive in with all the benefits of creating a laser-focused, deeply functional relationship with your personal style, let's face a few facts. Research says there is good cause to care how we look.

Looks and money, take 1. In a 1994 study by researchers at the University of Texas at Austin, and Michigan State University, 2,350 male and female executives were ranked by their attractiveness, as strikingly good-looking, above average, average, below average (plain), and homely (a slightly kinder word than *ugly*). The largest earners were those in the strikingly good-looking and above average categories, who earned 5 percent more than those who were deemed average and 10 percent more than those who were considered plain or homely.

Looks and money, take 2. Research from the University of Wisconsin shows that S&P 500 companies enjoy greater stock returns when they name new CEOs who are attractive. The researchers created a 10-point attractiveness scale and ran head shots of the 677 CEOs of S&P 500 companies through it. Analysis showed that when a new CEO took over, for each point on the attractiveness scale, a company showed (on average) a 1 percent boost in its stock price around that time.

Looks can hold us back. In 2016, Dove® soap surveyed 10,500 girls and women of all ages across 13 countries around the globe about body image and beauty. One of the company's findings: 85 percent of women and 79 percent of girls claim to opt out of important life activities—such as trying out for a team or club, asking for a raise, or engaging with family or loved ones—when they don't feel good about the way they look.

Obviously, when you are dissatisfied with the way you look, you spend enormous amounts of energy trying to either appear different or not appear at all. Sometimes, however, an important mindset shift can change your self-view: focus on who and what you are. Creating a wardrobe to celebrate your unique beauty is a powerful way to celebrate who you are.

THE WORKABLE WARDROBE

Chat with a personal organizer or a professional decluttering expert and you'll hear just how much trouble people have keeping their clothing in order. The problem is that most of us simply have too many things. Even if you tend toward the minimalist side of things, I bet you have at least two or three items you rarely (or never) wear. And you probably have several more that don't fit well, aren't flattering, or are in need of repair.

Danes and many Europeans have a simple system for curating their wardrobes. It works like this: create a core wardrobe of 15 to 25 high-quality, classic pieces (undergarments and athletic wear are separate) that you can accent with a few inexpensive trendy items each season. This has nothing to do with personal style—which will happen naturally for you if you choose items you love and that look good on you. This has to do with function, flattery, and ease.

A workable wardrobe looks something like this:

- One or two business-to-dressy skirts or dresses for women, or one or two pairs of work trousers, in neutral colors (no prints), for men
- One casual skirt for women, or one pair of casual trousers for men, in a neutral color
- Two blouses for women, or dress shirts for men, in neutral colors
- One to three T-shirts or other type of pullover shirts, in neutral colors
- One or two pairs of casual pants, such as khakis or jeans
- One or two pairs of business-to-dressy trousers
- One cardigan or pullover sweater
- One casual winter coat
- One business-to-dressy winter coat
- One pair business-to-dressy flats for women, or slip-on loafers for men
- One pair business-to-dressy pumps for women, or dress shoes for men
- One pair business-to-dressy boots
- One pair casual loafers or flats

Compare your wardrobe against the above list. Chances are, you already own many of these pieces. Where do you have gaps? Those are the places where you'll want to add items. Keep a list in your bag or on your phone so you can add core items to your wardrobe when you come across them.

And now for the other side of the hygge discussion: clearing out your closet.

I invite you to grab a piece of paper and a pen and stand in front of your closet. You are going to make an inventory. Ready?

Open your closet. Starting at the left of your hanging rod, list every single item, trying on each one and noting any stain or rip and remarking on how it fits. Use language like "Red blouse— good shape but very itchy; black silk dress—good shape, fits well; orange wool coat—too small in shoulders and arms too short." List as much as you can in one shot, but be flexible if you need to take a break. Come back to your list as soon as you can.

Assess other items. Once everything hanging on the main rod (or rods) is accounted for, move on to anything stacked on shelves above the closet, items hanging on hooks in the closet area, shoes on the floor, and so on. Then move on to your drawers, going from top to bottom. If you keep clothing anywhere else in the house—such as a front hall coat closet—list those items, too.

Get rid of damaged items. Grab a bag and immediately put everything with stains or irreparable rips into it. (Unless you are willing, at that very moment, to get out a needle and thread and mend any item. If you are not willing or able to repair the clothing immediately, put the item in the bag.) Place the bag out in your recycling bin. If your community does not yet recycle clothing, take it to a local recycling center or clothes-recycling kiosk. Otherwise, throw it in the trash.

Keep on discarding. Grab another bag and immediately put everything that does not fit into it. Then add anything that is itchy, uncomfortable, or unflattering—regardless of what you paid for it. Finally, go through what is left. This is your last chance to whittle down your wardrobe to a collection of strong core pieces. As you try on items, ask yourself: Do I enjoy wearing this? If you say no at any time, put that item in a giveaway bag.

Give it away. Take the bag—or bags—of items in good shape to your local thrift store. Do this quickly so you won't be tempted to fool yourself into keeping the items around to sell online. Chances are, you don't have time for this, and someone in your community could use these clothes right now.

To create a cozy, hygge-filled life, you will need to rein in your wardrobe, paring it down to items that look good on you and will work with others in your closet. Being able to grab and go is an enormous saver of time and energy. Further, focusing on quality and not quantity is liberating. Filling our closets with clutter (which is what cheap, ill-fitting clothing is) is not any different than filling our time or our lives with clutter: the cheap stuff finally overtakes the quality items, hiding them and making it hard for us to see the good that we have.

THE MYTH OF PERSONAL STYLE

Personal style is a bit of a myth. It's actually easy to develop. It takes two things: an unwillingness to wear items that don't flatter or feel right, regardless of how trendy or expensive, and a commitment to wearing only clothing that fits your body well (even if you have to take an item to a tailor for a shorter hem or a nip in the waistband). Both of these are very hygge-inspired attitudes. Among the Danish men and women I know, not one wears clothing that makes his or her body look misshapen. I have never seen one of these individuals sporting a piece that is too tight or too baggy in any area.

Interestingly, not one of these people dresses like another—I can always pick out a piece in a store window and say, "This jacket would suit so-and-so." That's because each human is drawn to different colors, fabrics, and cuts. A sensual friend favors tactile clothing that is fluffy or smooth with a soft silhouette. An artistic friend favors bolder lines and stronger colors. But what they share is they do not wear clothing that does not feel right for their personality, and they do not wear clothing that does not fit well. Day after day of dressing this way equals a personal style that is completely their own.

OVERCOMING OUTFIT BOREDOM

In past generations, people owned fewer clothes, so it was common to wear the same few items several times a week, or even every day. One of my grandmothers talked about washing her good blouse—her only good blouse—each evening so she could wear it the next day to her job as a schoolteacher.

Can you imagine doing that today? You may have a beloved shirt or pair of jeans you'd wear every day if you could—but you're stopped by the thought that people may notice you're wearing the same pants that you wore yesterday. The specter of other people's opinions is not the only thing that spurs you to create new outfits; there's also plain old boredom. Many of us take such pleasure in coming up with new looks that the idea of a workable wardrobe seems tedious.

Here are ideas to keep your wardrobe fun—without sacrificing your clean, calm, peaceful bedroom in order to buy more clothing.

Get trendy. Twice a year buy a few trendy accessories or less expensive pieces (an inexpensive shirt or pair of shoes that may only last a season) to keep your core wardrobe looking fresh. When the trend is over, they've served their purpose and can be either donated or recycled.

Rent it. Clothing rental services allow you to rent several pieces of clothing a month for a modest fee. With a subscription, you can rent a special occasion gown for that random black-tie dinner you were invited to, or a fun all-red ensemble for a Valentine's Day date, or try on a piece from a designer you've never worn before (a smart idea before investing in an expensive piece).

Hold a clothing swap. Each person brings a bag of like-new clothing—items that may have tags or be barely worn but just not right for that person. After organizing the items by size, you and your friends get to "shop" for things you love. One woman's cast-off is often another woman's perfect piece.

THE BEAUTY SYSTEM

Curtailing beauty product clutter will change your life. In relation to your home's other rooms, bathrooms are small and cramped. When they are cluttered with pots and brushes and bottles and wands, they look sloppy. Think about entering a bathroom that has smears of foundation on the sink, a stray smudge of eyeliner on a wall, towels stained with blush—not cozy or peaceful, is it?

A popular solution to beauty clutter is to purchase organizers or dedicate a closet to your collection. This does help keep things looking neat in the short term, but it doesn't help reduce the amount of stuff taking up space in your home. Do you really need five mascaras, regardless of how neatly they are stored?

Above I talked about how to create a workable clothing wardrobe. Here are some ideas for a manageable beauty product collection.

- Don't keep old makeup or skin-care products around. Not only do these items create clutter, but they could irritate your skin.

- Go through your hair-care, skin-care, and makeup products right now and toss anything you don't like or that doesn't help you. If you don't want to throw away an expensive item, reframe the situation: you've spent good money to house a product you don't use.

- Commit to one or two of an item in each category, including shampoo, conditioner, sunscreen, eye cream, mascara, foundation, and so forth. For instance, if you currently have more than two facial cleansers, use what you have and replace no more than two of them. Two different versions of each is quite generous.

- If you are addicted to beauty shopping, stop visiting beauty websites and reading beauty magazines. The less you focus on beauty products, the less strongly you'll feel like purchasing them.

- Sign up for a subscription beauty box. For a small fee, many beauty companies will send you a monthly box of skin-care, hair-care, or makeup samples that have been specially chosen to meet your specific needs. This is an easy way to try items before committing to a full-sized (and full-priced) item.

By following these steps, you'll discover easy ways to control the number of beauty products you bring into your home.

Most of us want every new product that comes out because we want to be as beautiful as possible. But what if we already see ourselves as beautiful? Could changing our mindset be enough to reduce the number of beauty products we buy?

One thing I love about my Danish friends and family is their absolute lack of vanity. They accept the way they look. A Danish woman will wear red lipstick because it is fun, but Danes don't spend an hour using contour to create the illusion of a thinner or fuller face, or highlighter to make the cheekbones look higher, or eye shadow to change the look of their eyes. It's just not part of the culture. As a result, Danes tend to see each other—and themselves— as wonderful as they are.

If you thought your hair, skin, and facial features were perfect as is, what products would you no longer need to use? If there are products that a perfect you would no longer need, could you try going without them for a month to see if they are worth keeping around?

The same theory applies to "natural-looking" makeup. From contour cream to highlighting powder to cover-up sticks to neutral-tinted lip gloss, the more you put on your face—and the more time you spend doing so—the more you are changing your appearance. That hour you spent giving yourself a "natural look" is an hour you cannot use in another way.

CAN HOMEMADE BEAUTY PRODUCTS CURE CLUTTER?

Making your own beauty products is a wonderful way to tame bathroom clutter. Made with fresh ingredients, homemade hair- and skin-care potions and cosmetics have a brief shelf life and must be made and used within a short period of time. This means no hanging around on a bathtub ledge, crowded into a medicine cabinet, or stashed under a bathroom sink. Homemade products also have other beautiful benefits that can help you create a cozy, warm feeling in your home. Focusing your intention on creating something wonderful for yourself (or another) is calming and leaves you feeling centered and happy. When that focus involves the sensual pleasures of silky oils and fragrances, even better! For anyone craving connection, crafting self-care products is a lovely activity to do with others: invite your family or friends to join you! Here are a few easy recipes to get you started.

WHIPPED COCONUT MOISTURIZER

I love this recipe. It's so luxurious, easy, and fun to make. It also makes an impressive gift. You'll need a stand mixer (or even a hand mixer) with a whisk attachment to make this moisturizer, as well as a small, sealable pot to store the cream. You can find these small containers at a craft store or any pharmacy—just look in the aisle where travel-sized toiletries are displayed. You can use this wonderful formula to moisturize your body as well as your hands—simply increase the amount of coconut oil you use and, if using, add more essential oils.

MAKES ABOUT ⅓ CUP

¼ cup coconut oil

Optional: 5 drops of your favorite essential oil

1. In the bowl of a stand mixer, using the whisk attachment, whip the coconut oil until light and fluffy.

2. Keep the mixer running and add the essential oil, if using, drop by drop.

3. Scrape the moisturizer into a sealable cosmetic pot and keep in a cool, dark place.

HOMEMADE SCRUB

This scrub uses natural ingredients to exfoliate, invigorate, and soften skin. It has the antibacterial, antimicrobial, and humectant benefits of both honey and coconut oil, creating a scrub that not only helps keep skin clear of break-outs but also softens and moisturizes at the same time.

MAKES ABOUT ¾ CUP

1 tablespoon coconut oil

2 tablespoons raw honey

Optional: 5 drops of your
favorite essential oil or oils

¼ cup sea salt

¼ cup organic sugar

1 tablespoon lemon juice

1. In a medium bowl, whisk together the coconut oil, honey, and essential oil(s), if using, set aside.

2. In another small bowl, blend the salt, sugar, and lemon juice until it becomes crumbly.

3. Pour the sugar mixture over the honey mixture and stir until smooth.

4. Scrape the scrub mixture into a sealable glass container.

STRAWBERRY-LEMON BRIGHTENING FACE MASK

I have always used homemade lemon masks to give my skin a bright glow and heal outbreaks. This is one of my favorites, thanks to strawberries, a terrific exfoliating and skin-healing ingredient—and it works well for all but the most sensitive skins.

MAKES ABOUT 2 TABLESPOONS

2 large strawberries

1 tablespoon lemon juice

1   In a bowl, mash together the strawberries and lemon juice with the back of a fork or a potato masher.

2. To use, start with clean skin and gently massage the mixture onto your face, neck, and décolleté. Leave on for 15 minutes before removing with cool water.

Note: Mask is for immediate use.

BLUEBERRY EYE PACK

Did you know that blueberries make great beauty treatments? This natural eye mask, based on blueberries and aloe, softens and firms, creating a relaxed, youthful look.

MAKES ABOUT 2 TABLESPOONS

2 tablespoons blueberries

½ tablespoon aloe vera juice (unflavored)

1. Add the ingredients to a food processor and pulse into a thick paste.

2. To use, apply the mixture to clean skin under and around the eyes. Leave on for 15 minutes before removing with cool water.

Note: Eye pack is for immediate use.

MOISTURIZING
CONDITIONING TREATMENT

This is an after-shampoo conditioner to use on the lower half of your hair. It isn't particularly oily, but because it contains some oil, I like to keep it away from the scalp. I have never tried this one on fine or thin hair—everyone in my family has a lot of hair, and this works well for us. So use this conditioner with that in mind. Also, this moisturizing treatment will not give your hair the slippery finish that many silicone-based commercial conditioners leave behind.

MAKES ABOUT ¼ CUP (ENOUGH FOR 1 USE)

¼ cup warm distilled water

½ teaspoon liquid coconut oil

¼ teaspoon sweet almond oil

5 drops of your favorite
   essential oil

1. In a blender, blend together all ingredients.

2. Pour the mixture into a jar or other covered container.

3. To use, shampoo hair as you would normally. Then apply the entire ¼ cup of conditioner to the bottom half of your hair, avoiding your scalp.

4. Allow the conditioner to work for 5 or more minutes, then rinse.

If you've been living in full-face makeup (or under a mane of product-enhanced hair) for several years, lightening up to allow the real you to shine through may leave you feeling a bit naked. If this is you, I sympathize. This was me, too, at one point. How I got comfy with my own skin: I pared down to one hair-styling product and three makeup items. This felt more comfortable than going "cold turkey." Then I branched out on a beauty limb and began going fresh-faced around the home, something I'd never done before. I began to see that I looked different without all the face paint. Not worse, but different. I was just as pretty sans cosmetics, but I looked more like me. Corny, I know, but true.

Hygge can give you a sense of comfort—and confidence—in your beauty. Remove the clutter that obscures your most stunning traits and see how easy and how much fun it is to be you.

ACKNOWLEDGMENTS

When I set out to write a book about hygge, that delightful type of Danish magic, I was apprehensive. I grew up with hygge and knew it inside and out, but for years and years I've been known as a healthy food and lifestyle author. Doing something new felt unsettling and (if I am truthful) scary. Fortunately, I have amazing friends who celebrated the creation of this beautiful book, walking with me every step of the way and cheering me on as I wrote.

A special thanks to my long-time head cheerleader, Oceana LeBlanc. Our morning check-ins are so powerful. They allow me to sit down to a day of writing with a sense of focus and fun. Lola, you were the one who truly understood what a big deal this book was to me and the one who celebrated everything from the finished manuscript to that first beautiful cover design. Thank you. Thank you, too, to Susan Clearwater for your interest in my work and your attention to my boys. Having you as an adult friend is an awesome thing and they always look forward to their time with you.

Speaking of my boys, I want to give a shout out to Leif, Anders, and Axel, my sons. As my children, you are used to the demands of living with a working writer. I appreciate your understanding around my deadlines and giving me the space I need to finish projects. As performers, you have a comfort with, and deep faith in, the creative process. You are learning how to navigate the ebbs and flows of motivation. And, you are learning how to surrender to the (sometimes uncomfy, often tedious) need to show up every single day, in order to both harness the power of inspiration and receive the beautiful gift of improvement. Creativity is our family business and watching your education in this area has been awe-inspiring. Thanks, too, to my husband, Richard Demler. You are a strong, steady, quiet anchor.

Thanks to my Danish family, the Pedersens and the Lunds, whose practical, warm, contented, comfortable way of viewing life felt like a warm comforter. The Hutchingses and Whipples—my American family—instilled in me an appreciation of tradition, food, human quirks, and the strength of family. Many of you, from each family, are now gone from this life. I miss you terribly, but you were generous enough to leave me with snug, pleasing, life-shaping memories; I call these memories up often.

I can't say enough complimentary things about my amazing editor, Meredith Hale. Full disclosure: I was not Meredith's easiest author in that I took *forever* to finish this book. (I am so sorry, Meredith!) But she handled my lengthy "book labor" with grace and good humor. My cover designer, Elizabeth Mihaltse Lindy, and interior designer, Gavin Motnyk, ensured that this book is as beautiful and "cozy-looking" as it is! Mitch Blunt created the perfect hygge art for *American Cozy*. And our very thorough copy editors, Lori Paximadis, Kathy Brock, and Renee Yewdaev, ensured that the facts I shared and research I cited was correct, while smoothing out unclear language and anything else that got in the way of creating the best book possible.

Lastly, I must thank you, dear reader, for your interest in creating a cozy, hygge-filled life. This may be one of the happiest things you do for yourself and those around you. Have fun!

Much love,
Stephanie

BIBLIOGRAPHY

Alberti, Marina. "Measuring Urban Sustainability." *Environmental Impact Assessment Review*, no. 16 (1996): 381–424.

American Psychological Association. *Stress in America: Missing the Health Care Connection.* February 7, 2013. http://www.apa.org/news/press /releases/stress/2012/full-report.pdf.

Anderson, G. Oscar. "Loneliness among Older Adults: A National Survey of Adults 45+." Washington, DC: AARP Research, September 2010. https: //doi.org/10.26419/res.00064.001.

Ansell, Emily B., Kenneth Rando, Keri Tuit, Joseph Guarnaccia, and Rajita Sinha. "Cumulative Adversity and Smaller Gray Matter Volume in Medial Prefrontal, Anterior Cingulate, and Insula Regions." *Biological Psychiatry* 72, no. 1 (July 1, 2012): 57–64. http://www .biologicalpsychiatryjournal.com/article/S0006-3223(11)01193-0/fulltext.

Arnold, Jeanne E., and Ursula A. Lang. "Changing American Home Life: Trends in Domestic Leisure and Storage among Middle-Class Families." *Journal of Family Economic Issues* 23 (March 28, 2007). https://link.springer.com /article/10.1007%2Fs10834-006-9052-5.

Buchanan, Kathryn E., and Anat Bardi. "Acts of Kindness and Acts of Novelty Affect Life Satisfaction." *Journal of Social Psychology* 1050, no. 3 (August 10, 2010): 235–237. https://doi.org/10.1080/00224540903365554.

Campbell, Emma. "The Daily Worth Value of a Woman's Face." SkinStore. March 2017. http://www.skinstore.com/blog/skincare/womens-face -worth-survey-2017.

Crooks, Ross. "Beauty or Bust: Obsessed with Cosmetics." MintLife (blog). April 11, 2013. https://blog.mint.com/consumer-iq/splurge-vs-save-which-beauty-products-are-worth-the-extra-cost-0413.

"Dogs Ease Anxiety, Improve Health Status of Hospitalized Heart Failure Patients." American Heart Association Abstract 2513. November 15, 2005. https://www.uclahealth.org/pac/Workfiles/volunteering/PACArticle.pdf.

Grabmeier, Jeff. "Lousy Jobs Hurt Your Health by the Time You're in Your 40s." Ohio State News. August 22, 2016. https://news.osu.edu/news/2016/08/22/lousy-jobs.

Halford, Joseph Taylor, and Scott H. C. Hsu. "Beauty Is Wealth: CEO Appearance and Shareholder Value" (December 19, 2014). Available at SSRN: http://dx.doi.org/10.2139/ssrn.2357756.

Haviland-Jones, Jeannette, Holly Hale Rosario, Patricia Wilon, and Terry R. McGuire. "An Environmental Approach to Positive Emotion: Flowers." *Evolutionary Psychology* 3, no. 1 (January 1, 2005). http://journals.sagepub.com/doi/10.1177/147470490500300109.

Helliwell, J., R. Layard, and J. Sachs. "World Happiness Report." New York: Sustainable Development Solutions Network, 2017. http://worldhappiness.report.

"Is a Marker of Preclinical Alzheimer's Disease Associated with Loneliness?" *Science Daily*, November 2, 2016. www.sciencedaily.com/releases/2016/11/161102132631.htm.

Kilpatrick, L. A., B. Y. Suyenobu, S. R. Smith, J.A. Bueller, T. Goodman, J. D. Creswell, K. Tillisch, E. A. Mayer, and B. D. Naliboff. "Impact of Mindfulness-Based Stress Reduction Training on Intrinsic Brain Connectivity." *Neuroimage* 56, no. 1 (May 1, 2011): 290–298. https://www.ncbi.nlm.nih.gov/pubmed/21334442.

LeRoy, Angie S., Kyle W. Murdock, Lisa M. Jaremka, Asad Loya, and Christopher P. Fagundes. "Loneliness Predicts Self-Reported Cold Symptoms after a Viral Challenge." *Health Psychology* 36, no. 5 (May 2017): 512–520. doi: 10.1037/hea0000467.

McMains, S., and S. Kastner. "Interactions of Top-Down and Bottom-Up Mechanisms in Human Visual Cortex." *Journal of Neuroscience* 31, no. 2 (January 12, 2011): 587–597. https://www.ncbi.nlm.nih.gov/pubmed/21228167.

Meeker, Mary. "Internet Trends Report." Kleiner Perkins Caufield and Byers. http://www.kpcb.com/internet-trends.

Ophir, Eyal, Clifford Nass, and Anthony D. Wagner. "Cognitive Control in Media Multitaskers." *Proceedings of the National Academy of Sciences* 106, no. 37 (September 2009): 15583–15587.

Organisation for Economic Co-operation and Development. "Average Usual Weekly Hours Worked on the Main Job." OECD.Stat. https://stats.oecd.org/Index.aspx?DataSetCode=AVE_HRS.

Palouzier-Paulignan, Brigitte, Marie-Christine Lacroix, Pascaline Aimé, Christine Baly, Monique Caillol, Patrice Congar, A. Karyn Julliard, Kristal Tucker, and Debra Ann Fadool. "Olfaction under Metabolic Influences." *Chemical Senses* 37, no. 9 (November 2012): 769–797. https://academic.oup.com/chemse/article/37/9/769/326102.

Paugam-Burtz, Catherine, and Jean Mantz. "Sedative Effects of Mozart's Music in the Critically Ill: Enjoy the Hormonal Symphony." *Critical Care Medicine* 35, no. 12 (December 2007): 2858–2859. https://journals.lww.com /ccmjournal/Citation/2007/12000/Sedative_effects_of_Mozart_s_music_in _the.29.aspx.

"People at Risk of Hoarding Disorder May Have Serious Complaints about Sleep." ScienceDaily. June 8, 2015. www.sciencedaily.com /releases/2015/06/150608213030.htm.

Radicati, Sara. "Email Statistics Report, 2014–2018." Radicati Group. http: //www.radicati.com/wp/wp-content/uploads/2014/01/Email-Statistics -Report-2014-2018-Executive-Summary.pdf.

Schoenfeld, Timothy J., Pedro Rada, Pedro R. Pieruzzini, Brian Hsueh, and Elizabeth Gould. "Physical Exercise Prevents Stress-Induced Activation of Granule Neurons and Enhances Local Inhibitory Mechanisms in the Dentate Gyrus." *Journal of Neuroscience* 33, no. 18 (May 1, 2013): 7770–7777. http://www.jneurosci.org/content/33/18/7770.

Shakya, H. B., and N. A. Christakis. "Association of Facebook Use with Compromised Well-Being: A Longitudinal Study." *American Journal of Epidemiology* 185, no. 3 (February 1, 2017): 203–211. https://www.ncbi.nlm .nih.gov/pubmed/28093386.

Sin, Nancy L., Jennifer E. Graham-Engeland, and David M. Almeida. "Daily Positive Events and Inflammation: Findings from the National Study of Daily Experiences." *Brain Behavior and Immunity* 45 (January 2015): 130–138. https://www.sciencedirect.com/science/article/pii /S0889159114004073.

Unilever Corporation. "The Dove Global Beauty and Confidence Report." June 23, 2016. https://www.unilever.com/Images/global-beauty-confidence -report-infographic_tcm244-501412_en.pdf.

Vartanian, Lenny R., Kristin M. Kernan, and Brian Wansink. "Clutter, Chaos, and Overconsumption: The Role of Mind-Set in Stressful and Chaotic Food Environments." *Environment and Behavior* 49, no. 2 (February 1, 2017): 215–223. http://journals.sagepub.com/doi/abs/10.1177/0013916516628178.

Wu, Ming, José Carlos Pastor-Pareja, and Tian Xu. "Interaction between *Ras*V12 and *Scribble* Clones Induces Tumour Growth and Invasion." *Nature* 463, no. 7280 (January 28, 2010): 545–548. https://www.ncbi.nlm .nih.gov/pmc/articles/PMC2835536.

FURTHER READING

Adarme, Adrianna. *The Year of Cozy: 125 Recipes, Crafts and Other Homemade Adventures* (Rodale Books, 2015).

Allen, Katherine. *Emily's Room: Creating Spaces That Unlock Your Potential* (Tru Publishing, 2015).

Bentsen, Lena. *Goodbye Clutter, Hello Freedom: How to Create Space for Danish Hygge and Lifestyle by Cleaning up, Organizing and Decorating with Care* (Lena Bentsen Publishing, 2016).

David, Deborah Schoeberlein. *Living Mindfully: At Home, at Work, and in the World* (Wisdom Publications, 2015).

Doré, Garance. *Love Style Life* (Spiegel & Grau, 2015).

Kondo, Marie. *The Life-Changing Magic of Tidying Up: The Japanese Art of Decluttering and Organizing* (Ten Speed Press, 2014).

Maushart Susan. *The Winter of Our Disconnect: How One Family Pulled the Plug and Lived to Tell/Text/Tweet the Tale* (Profile Books, 2012).

Mitchell, Emma. *Making Winter: A Hygge-Inspired Guide to Surviving the Winter Months* (Lark Crafts, 2017).

Nettleton, Sarah. *The Simple Home: The Luxury of Enough* (Taunton Press, 2007).

Smith, Michael S. *The Curated House: Creating Style, Beauty, and Balance* (Rizzoli, 2015).

INDEX

ABOUT THE AUTHOR

S tephanie Pedersen is a lifestyle expert and author who loves all things American cozy and all things hygge. As the daughter of an American and a Dane, Stephanie grew up enjoying the blessings and teachings of both cultures.

She is raising her own three children—Leif, Anders, and Axel—in her adopted hometown of New York City, a city of 8.5 million people, small homes, and constant busyness, which offers enormous opportunity to both practice and teach her sons the decluttering, homemaking, sane scheduling, and mood-transforming lessons of her childhood.

(continued on next page)

Stephanie is the author of several cookbooks, including *Kale: The Complete Guide to the World's Most Powerful Superfood, Coconut: The Complete Guide to the World's Most Versatile Superfood, Berries: The Complete Guide to Cooking with Power-Packed Berries, The 7-Day Superfood Cleanse,* and *Roots: The Complete Guide to the Underground Superfood,* all published by Sterling Publishing Co., Inc.

You can find Stephanie online at www.StephaniePedersen.com, where you can read more about how she creates her own version of American cozy. You'll find recipes, photos, tutorials, strategies, and more for creating a sane, productive, comfort-filled life. You can also access episodes of Stephanie's radio shows and podcasts, read chapters of her cookbooks, and offer your own feedback.

You can also find Stephanie at:

www.stephaniepedersen.com/podcast
www.StephaniePedersenBooks.com
YouTube: www.YouTube.com/StephaniePedersenTV
Facebook: www.facebook.com/PedersenSteph
Twitter: @StPedersen
Pinterest: StPedersen
Instagram: stephaniepedersenlovesyou
LinkedIn: http://www.linkedin.com/in/stephaniepedersen